Praise for *Firefighter Zen*

"Wise and practical, simple yet profound, *Firefighter Zen* is filled with tales of everyday endurance and frailty. As a parish minister (and first responder) acquainted with grief and healing, I highly recommend this field guide to negotiating life's alarums with calm, clarity, and courage."
— **Reverend Gary Kowalski,** author of *Goodbye, Friend: Healing Wisdom for Anyone Who Has Ever Lost a Pet*

"Hersch Wilson's deceptively simple mantra — be brave, be kind, fight fires — contains not only great wisdom but also a call to action. The internal peace you're looking for is to be found by serving others out in the world. This book left me both revitalized and inspired."
— **Brian Castner,** author of *The Long Walk: A Story of War and the Life That Follows*

"*Firefighter Zen* is one of those rare books that draws on firsthand experience and ageless wisdom to convey life's immutable lessons. Hersch Wilson uses clean, elegant prose to tell stories that are at times light, dark, funny, tragic, and compelling, and always instructive. This book is a must-read not only for anyone in a profession required to answer emergencies but for all of us who at times experience life's unrelenting, tragic, and sublime beauty and want to think more deeply about it."
— **Cary Johns Griffith,** author of *Gunflint Burning: Fire in the Boundary Waters* and *Lost in the Wild: Danger and Survival in the North Woods*

"Hersch Wilson's *Firefighter Zen* is an up-close-and-personal look at the courage, humanity, and great heart required of those among us referred to as first responders. Deeply compassionate and wise, this book belongs on the shelves of all those who respond to the world of tragedy, their hearts filled with the wisdom of service to others. This book is a beacon of light not only for first responders but for all of us striving to live more meaningful lives. As an engaging testament to how important it is to be strong, to be brave, and to keep showing up, *Firefighter Zen* contains numerous stories that will take you into the heart of a greatness and grief you may have always admired but not clearly

umping Fire: ting Wildfire

"This beautiful memoir of the experiences of a volunteer firefighter in New Mexico is a page-turner that also happens to be packed with wisdom. Author Hersch Wilson is an exquisite storyteller who writes in succinct, engaging, evocative prose. *Firefighter Zen*'s stories of suffering, courage, drama, humor, and triumph are organized not chronologically but rather into a set of tightly connected lessons for living life well. I kept worrying that each next chapter could not possibly live up to the standard set by the ones that came before, but the book never disappoints; story after story is pitch-perfect. It is astonishingly good."

— **Amy C. Edmondson,** professor at Harvard Business School
and author of *The Fearless Organization*

"Inspiring, helpful, deeply meaningful, and moving. Much more than a practical guide for maintaining health, peace, and wellness during the trials of life, *Firefighter Zen* is also a testament to living a life of fulfillment by finding purpose through compassionate service, mercy, and usefulness to others."

— **Police Capt. Dan Willis** (ret.), author of *Bulletproof Spirit:
The First Responder's Essential Resource for Protecting
and Healing Mind and Heart*

"Gripping, eloquent, and insightfully written, *Firefighter Zen* offers an inside glimpse into the unpredictable and chaotic life of a firefighter, reminding us there is no safety in avoidance and the best way out is always through. Full of heart-pounding 911 calls and timeless spiritual truths, Wilson's book describes the many challenges and intense hardships firefighters and EMTs endure, but also offers a blueprint on how to thrive, maintain our humanity, and find transcendence on the other side. And with first responder PTSD and 'mental injury' at an all-time high, this beautifully crafted book is as nourishing as a cool oasis in a stark desert."

— **Kevin Grange,** author of *Lights & Sirens:
The Education of a Paramedic*

firefighter zen

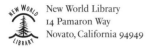 New World Library
14 Pamaron Way
Novato, California 94949

The material in this book is intended for education. It is not meant to take the place of diagnosis and treatment by a qualified medical practitioner or therapist. No expressed or implied guarantee of the effects of the use of the recommendations can be given or liability taken.

Text design by Tona Pearce Myers

Library of Congress Cataloging-in-Publication Data

Names: Wilson, Hersch, author.
Title: Firefighter zen : a field guide to thriving in tough times / Hersch Wilson.
Description: Novato, California : New World Library, [2020] | Summary: "Drawing on decades of experience, a volunteer firefighter discusses the mental habits that allow firefighters to maintain their sanity in the face of danger and tragedy. Finding analogies with Zen practice, the author shows readers how to apply these same habits to the inevitable difficulties of daily life."-- Provided by publisher.
Identifiers: LCCN 2020004772 (print) | LCCN 2020004773 (ebook) | ISBN9781608686889 (paperback ; alk. paper) | ISBN 9781608686896 (epub)
Subjects: LCSH: Wilson, Hersch. | Fire fighters--Psychology. | Fires--Psychological aspects. | Conduct of life.
Classification: LCC TH9118.W557 A3 2020 (print) | LCC TH9118.W557 (ebook) | DDC 363.3701/9--dc23
LC record available at https://lccn.loc.gov/2020004772
LC ebook record available at https://lccn.loc.gov/2020004773

First printing, May 2020
ISBN 978-1-60868-688-9
Ebook ISBN 978-1-60868-689-6
Printed in Canada on 100% postconsumer-waste recycled paper

 New World Library is proud to be a Gold Certified Environmentally Responsible Publisher. Publisher certification awarded by Green Press Initiative.

10   9   8   7   6   5   4   3   2

This book is dedicated first to my wife and firefighter partner, Laurie. Next, a shout-out to my daughters, Brynne and Sully. They have spent their lifetimes listening to pagers ring out and having conversations, dinners, and movies suspended by 911 calls.

Finally, a toast to the "old guys" in the department and the work they've done for decades to keep their community safe.

Part 3: When Dragons Come   103

Chapter 14: Something Is Coming Toward Us   107
Chapter 15: Stay Inside the Hula Hoop   115
Chapter 16: Get Under the Smoke   125
Chapter 17: The Dragon Fire   131
Chapter 18: We Are Not Superheroes   141

Part 4: The Grief Road   149

Chapter 19: The Midnight Call   153
Chapter 20: The Next Few Months Are Gonna Suck   163
Chapter 21: When the Caring Comes Back   169
Chapter 22: I Will Never Be the Same,
   But I Will Get Better   173

Part 5: Be Brave. Be Kind. Fight Fires.   181

Chapter 23: Be Brave   185
Chapter 24: Be Kind   193
Chapter 25: Be Useful   203
Chapter 26: Belong   213
Chapter 27: Be Tough   221
Chapter 28: The Blue-Hazed Prairie   229

Epilogue: The Oldest Fire Department in the West   235
Acknowledgments   241
About the Author   243

CONTENTS

The Joy of Firefighting   *xiii*
Why a Field Guide   *xv*
Introduction: First Call   *1*

Part 1: The Firefighter Universe   11

Chapter 1: I Can't Die, I'm Booked…   15
Chapter 2: The Glitch   21
Chapter 3: God, Chaos, and Firefighters   27
Chapter 4: So, Death   33
Chapter 5: Cowboy Kicked by Dead Cow   41
Chapter 6: Rites of Passage   49
Chapter 7: On Dying   61

Part 2: Keep Calm and Carry On   65

Chapter 8: Adrenaline Junkies   69
Chapter 9: The Eighty-Seventh Problem   73
Chapter 10: Emergencies, Problems, and Inconveniences   79
Chapter 11: Not My Emergency   87
Chapter 12: The Zen of Firefighting   93
Chapter 13: Staying Calm: A Primer   97

tho'
We are not now that strength which in old days
Moved earth and heaven, that which we are, we are;
One equal temper of heroic hearts,
Made weak by time and fate, but strong in will
To strive, to seek, to find, and not to yield.

— ALFRED, LORD TENNYSON, "Ulysses"

THE JOY OF FIREFIGHTING

We had a car crash in the middle of an autumn night. We were a little ramped up because the call had gone out "young children involved." As I drove to the scene, I felt anxiety building. There was that sinking feeling that this would be another bad call. I got there, saw the wrecked car, checked in with command, and was assigned patient care for one of the young girls. The chief told me that she was about eight years old, status unknown. I jogged down to the car, buckling my bunker jacket. I opened the car door and saw the little girl, who appeared uninjured but teary-eyed. I said, "Hi, my name is Hersch. I'm with the fire department. Are you okay?" In response, she just leaped into my arms, almost knocking me over. I was so relieved. She tightly held on to me, and I carried her across the median to the waiting ambulance. She was fine, and I thought, *Best call ever!*

It was such a simple thing. Not the most dramatic, nor the most memorable, emergency of my thirty-plus years as a firefighter, but one that sums up the joy that can come from first responding. There is darkness, tragedy, and suffering, to be sure. But every once in a while, a child leaps into your arms. And at that moment, you know you are doing the work you are meant to do, and that feeling is joy.

This is the thesis of this book. Life brings with it anxiety, suffering, and tragedy; stuff happens. The world feels a mess. Our lives turn on that dime. Yet we each have the ability and the capacity to find joy.

Here is the promise of this book. If we accept life for what it is, with no illusions, if we can keep our perspective when all around us individuals are losing theirs, if we take as fact that we will suffer and grieve, and finally, if we deeply commit to the understanding that the highest calling is service to others, then we have a shot at finding joy.

This is what being a volunteer firefighter has taught me, and I want to share these lessons with you.

Be brave. Be kind. Fight fires.

FIRST CALL

> What do we live for, if it is not to make life less
> difficult to each other?
>
> — GEORGE ELIOT, *Middlemarch*

Early on a Tuesday evening in November 1986, my wife, Laurie, and I became volunteer firefighters. After six months of training, we were voted into the Hondo Volunteer Fire Department and given permission to respond to calls.

We went home, congratulated each other, had dinner, and began doing the dishes. At about 9:30 PM, we suddenly heard this horrendous, high-pitched shriek.

"Holy shit, what was that?" Laurie yelled. We looked at each other and then noticed that both of our fire department pagers — which we would carry with us 24/7 for the next several decades, and which would largely run our lives — were vibrating on the kitchen counter. An unintelligible voice came over the radio: "Hondo — *crackle, crackle* — car fire — *crackle, crackle*."

"Wait," Laurie exclaimed. "They're going to page us *at night?*"

We momentarily put aside Laurie's critical insight as we tried to remember what we were supposed to do. Completely adrenalized — *a car on fire!* — I asked, "What should I wear? Who's going to drive? Where are the dogs?"

We managed to settle down, get the dogs inside the house, and get ourselves out of it. We jumped into our old and cranky Nissan Pathfinder and headed toward our first call.

This was our induction into the vocation and, to Laurie's dismay, the realization that, yes, they were going to page us at night. There would be many such nights, followed by countless exhausted mornings and coffee-laden hours at our day jobs. Yet as soon as we opened the door that first night and headed toward the fire, we knew these physical inconveniences weren't going to matter. We were hooked. While a little concerned by the disruption we had invited into our lives, we were both thrilled and sobered by the understanding that our worldview was about to irrevocably change.

Our story of joining a volunteer fire department is one shared all over the country. There are approximately 1.2 million firefighters in the United States. Of that number, 70 percent are volunteers. Of the sixty firefighter deaths in 2017, thirty-two were volunteers. Although major cities have paid firefighters (we call them "career" firefighters), medium-sized cities, small towns, suburbs, and rural America are served by largely volunteer or combined (career and volunteer) departments. The volunteer fire department dates back to the first fire brigade founded by none other than Benjamin Franklin in Philadelphia in 1736.

Joining a volunteer fire department was not my idea. Laurie and I were in our thirties and settled in our ways. Also, I was never one of those kids who watched the seventies' TV show *Emergency!* and dreamed about being a firefighter or an EMT. The idea was Laurie's. She worked at a conference center outside of Santa Fe. One summer evening, a guest fell and broke her ankle. There was no one trained in first aid to help, and Laurie had to struggle to treat the woman. She vowed never to let that happen again. She signed up and completed a six-month emergency medical technician course. At the end of the course, the instructor asked if she would be interested in joining a fire department — just to keep her skills fresh. She thought it was a great idea and came home and tried to sell me on it. I resisted. I couldn't see myself with an ax breaking down doors, and I had a "thing" about blood and gore. But she persisted and we went to that first meeting. I almost fainted when the gathered firefighters passed around a picture of a deceased car-crash victim with a broken neck — but Laurie was intrigued. Seeing my discomfort, she whispered in my ear, "Maybe you can just learn how to run the engines..."

And that is how we became firefighters. Laurie dove in enthusiastically. I was more reluctant. But after a few months, I became as excited as she was.

Before we joined the department, Laurie and I had led insular lives. Unlike most firefighters, we'd both begun our adulthoods as dancers in the cloistered world of ballet. By its nature, ballet is an all-consuming enterprise. Dancers are extremely focused, seeing only the studio, the theater, and their career paths. When we retired from dance, we jumped right into jobs, but we still saw life as if we were wearing blinders. Our sense of what was going on in our town and even in our neighborhood was at best an abstraction, brought to us by the news or occasional gossip at work.

We helped pull the doors off the burning van, and for the first time, we got to use a hose line to extinguish a real fire.

At the end, we carried hoses on our shoulders back to the engines and helped pack them. Back at the station, all the equipment — axes, nozzles, radios — were cleaned, recharged, and put back on the right vehicles.

show *Emergency!* and dreamed about being a firefighter or an EMT. The idea was Laurie's. She worked at a conference center outside of Santa Fe. One summer evening, a guest fell and broke her ankle. There was no one trained in first aid to help, and Laurie had to struggle to treat the woman. She vowed never to let that happen again. She signed up and completed a six-month emergency medical technician course. At the end of the course, the instructor asked if she would be interested in joining a fire department — just to keep her skills fresh. She thought it was a great idea and came home and tried to sell me on it. I resisted. I couldn't see myself with an ax breaking down doors, and I had a "thing" about blood and gore. But she persisted and we went to that first meeting. I almost fainted when the gathered firefighters passed around a picture of a deceased car-crash victim with a broken neck — but Laurie was intrigued. Seeing my discomfort, she whispered in my ear, "Maybe you can just learn how to run the engines…"

And that is how we became firefighters. Laurie dove in enthusiastically. I was more reluctant. But after a few months, I became as excited as she was.

Before we joined the department, Laurie and I had led insular lives. Unlike most firefighters, we'd both begun our adulthoods as dancers in the cloistered world of ballet. By its nature, ballet is an all-consuming enterprise. Dancers are extremely focused, seeing only the studio, the theater, and their career paths. When we retired from dance, we jumped right into jobs, but we still saw life as if we were wearing blinders. Our sense of what was going on in our town and even in our neighborhood was at best an abstraction, brought to us by the news or occasional gossip at work.

Was there suffering? Were tragedies happening? Of course. But because they didn't have an immediate impact on our lives, they were rarely on our radar. For most of our twenties and thirties, we thought that life was, at worst, benign.

I would argue that most of us are similarly afflicted. I don't mean this pejoratively. We grapple with work and family, with hardly a moment to think, reflect, or observe. We live in the most politically charged times since the sixties. The oxygen is daily sucked out of the room by the next crisis and the next. All this swirls around us and distracts us from what the writer H.G. Wells called the "primary and elemental necessities" of life.

For Laurie and me, becoming volunteer firefighters brought those elemental and primal aspects of living sharply into focus. From the night we received that first page, we were tossed into a world of fires, car crashes, and cardiac arrests. With words that were never adequate, we were asked to comfort individuals who were suffering, who'd just lost someone or were themselves terrified of dying. We saw that "calls" — the firefighter's term for someone in trouble — don't discriminate. It doesn't matter how busy you might be or how successful or beloved you are. A banker, thinking of the day's schedule, falls to the floor in a Starbucks, clutching his chest. A couple holds each other outside their double-wide as it explodes in flame. A teenage son lies in the bathtub facedown in the water, half his body blue, heroin paraphernalia on the sink. A homeless man curls lifeless in a snowdrift, his arm defiantly sticking out of the melting snow. Firefighting quickly tossed and scrambled our assumptions about living — and about our own lives. Our notions of security became more tenuous. We had to come to grips with the fact that suffering and pain were all around us. We had to accept the emerging truth: The one promise the universe makes and keeps is that we will experience tragedy.

The inevitability of disaster soon becomes part of the firefighter's DNA. But somehow most firefighters I know are resolutely good-humored and composed; it's hard to fluster a good firefighter. We have learned how to thrive here, in this universe of uncertain futures and certain tragedy.

We learn to thrive *because of* the calamity and heartbreak we see almost every day; not, as people often think, *despite* what we experience. Laurie and I, and most volunteer firefighters we know, have stumbled on a heart-saving secret. When we accept the reality that society is just a veneer that masks the fundamental drumbeats of an immutable and uncaring universe, our path to fulfillment is straight toward calamity. When we serve, when we take care of strangers, when we work in community to save a community, we feel most alive. This isn't an adrenaline rush, although there's that, too; it's mostly in the shift from "me-centered" to "other-centered" that we find meaning and even joy.

You don't have to be a firefighter to find that fulfillment. You just have to see the world through a firefighter's eyes.

Back to that first call. Laurie and I drove to scene. Lights and strobes from the engines were still flashing. The crackle of the radio was loud, and there was the acrid smell of smoke and burning plastic in the air.

The ten or so Hondo firefighters, men and women, were all wearing bunker gear; black pants and bunker coats, black helmets and gloves. Dan, the chief, waved us over and put us to work.

We helped pull the doors off the burning van, and for the first time, we got to use a hose line to extinguish a real fire.

At the end, we carried hoses on our shoulders back to the engines and helped pack them. Back at the station, all the equipment — axes, nozzles, radios — were cleaned, recharged, and put back on the right vehicles.

We were ready for the next call, whatever it might be. By the time we were done, it was near midnight. But there was nothing but the smiles and laughter of a group of friends and neighbors doing important work. Such is the way of volunteer fire departments.

We both got a few hours of sleep that night. The next morning, I woke up and realized that for most of my adult life, although I enjoyed work, and had a great life, it often felt as if something was missing. That first call, the first time we responded, was as if the tumblers in the universe clicked into place for me. I had found what I was meant to be: a volunteer firefighter.

Truthfully, a few hours later at my desk, the aura had faded and I found myself napping at work. (Drooling, I recall, was involved.) I wasn't quite yet adjusted to sleep deprivation. That would come later. But on that day, I knew we were on the path to something important.

Decades have flown by since that first call. We have two daughters, who spent many a school night doing homework at the fire station. We learned how to balance raising kids and running on calls. I ultimately became an EMT because, like in the rest of the country, the vast number of calls we go on are medical emergencies. (I mostly got over the blood and gore phobia!)

Laurie retired after twenty years. I'm still hanging in going into my third decade — something I never would have imagined when we were dancers.

But that is how it all works, right? You can have plans, but life turns out to be a wild and unpredictable ride. If I could have given any cryptic advice to my eighteen-year-old self, it would have been, "Hang on."

The Volunteer Life

It will help to know a little bit about the volunteer firefighter life. The department we joined, Hondo Volunteer Fire and Rescue, sits just east of Santa Fe, New Mexico. Sort of suburban, but also wild and rural. Coyotes howl in the night when they hear our sirens. It was founded in 1974. At any given time, there are anywhere from fifteen to thirty members. When we began responding, the department ran on about two hundred calls a year. In 2017, we ran on a little over five hundred calls. Approximately 80 percent of our calls are medical, 15 percent or so are car crashes, and the rest are fires. Most calls are not big emergencies but rather anything from helping an elderly patient who has fallen get back into bed to diabetic problems; some patients use the ambulance as a "taxi" to get to the hospital. We're a small fire department, but busy.

We have two stations, two fire engines, one heavy-rescue truck (that carries the "jaws of life" and a host of other rescue tools), two tenders (that deliver water to fires in rural areas that have no hydrants), two wildland fire engines, and one ambulance.

Reflecting Santa Fe, our membership runs the political

gamut. We've had socialists, an anarchist, left-leaning members, and right-leaning, all the way to gun-toting "live free or die" conservatives: all joined by the common cause of saving people. The department is composed of lawyers, contractors, realtors, teachers, artists, one federal judge, and business-folks.

Hondo firefighters are trained to fight structure fires and wildland fires and to deal with vehicle crashes, and the EMTs are trained to manage all sorts of medical emergencies, from trauma to cardiac arrests and overdoses.

When the pager tones out (a 911 call), members drop whatever they are doing, leave the office or home (or get out of bed), and either go to the station to pick up trucks or drive directly to the scene of the call. Some members have emergency lights and sirens in their vehicles; we all have fire department radios.

Volunteers are essentially "on call" twenty-four hours a day, seven days a week, which can lead to lots of disruption of normal life.

Finally, volunteers in our department receive the same training and are subject to the same certifications as career firefighters. As we say, a fire doesn't care if you are volunteer or career; it takes experience and training to fight it.

It is a lot of work, but the payoffs are those illusive twins, passion and fulfillment. To paraphrase my favorite line from the movie *A League of Their Own*, about baseball, "It's the hard that makes it great."

part one

THE FIREFIGHTER UNIVERSE

It's philosophy's job to eviscerate
our happiness.

— REBECCA GOLDSTEIN

It's probably not the most inviting opening to this book, intimating that your happiness will be eviscerated. Trust me, that isn't the goal.

Rather, the goal of part 1 — as in every beginning — is to provide a deep and abiding grasp of how things work. I don't mean the science of the universe, but the rules of existence that directly apply to us as individuals living today in our astonishingly comfortable "first world" (as compared to the last hundred thousand years or so).

The philosophical argument I make is that firefighters have a unique perspective on what the rules are and how they apply to us.

It's a simple premise. By the nature of our vocation, we see life in extremis. We care for people in their worst and often life-defining moments. You can't help but walk away from those calls with an unmuddled sense of how things work.

That clarity is what I want to provide.

The core idea is that when we accept the rules for what they are, when we accept the universe for what it is rather than for what we wish it were, then we have a shot at finding fulfillment and joy.

But to reach that place, that clarity, our happiness must endure some eviscerating.

CHAPTER ONE

I CAN'T DIE, I'M BOOKED...

Our greatest mistake is believing we have time.

— BUDDHA

In his eighties, the legendary vaudeville comedian George Burns once quipped, "I can't die, I'm booked."

There is such sweetness in that joke because it is telling of how we all think. We're busy, our thoughts are on today and maybe next year. We have stuff to do, schedules to keep. We have too much going on to think about our deaths, much less to actually die.

To most of us death is an abstraction, an event a "lifetime" away, something that shouldn't influence what we do today.

Being a firefighter — being continually exposed to death and to the suddenness with which it often comes — changes that point of view.

We live in a universe — the firefighter universe — where any 911 call might be a death. Death by trauma, overdoses, medical causes, and suicide are the lingua franca of first responding.

The indelible lesson from this is not that death is inevitable but rather its corollary, our time here is short.

This is cathartic knowledge. It changes how you see time. It changes how you view your life.

More than once after a bad call — such as after a cardiac arrest — when I've stepped back into the non–fire department world, with its everyday problems, with its politics and its jostling for status, I've thought about Ralph Waldo Emerson's advice that "sometimes a scream is better than a thesis." I've wanted to shout, "Stop what you're doing! Is what you're doing important? You don't have time to waste! Don't be afraid! Hold your children, tell great stories! Take care of people, smash the glasses against the wall!"

I can't give you that experience, but maybe this exercise will be of assistance.

Your Lifeline

Draw a line across a blank sheet of paper. On the left end of the line, write the year you were born. Simple, right?

Now, on the right end of the line, write the year you will die. Not so simple.

There's a lot of denial and maybe some anxiety about that particular date. But the fact is, you will die, and it will happen on a specific date. That date will be as concrete and real as the day you were born.

To estimate it, use the length of time your parents or grandparents lived. This rule of thumb will be a guess, a bet with the universe, but the odds are you'll be close. Even if you're off by a bit, just identifying the age you might die will grab your attention.

Use that age to figure out the year of your death. Write that year down.

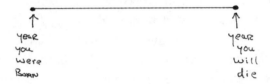

This "lifeline" represents your life from birth to death. Since what is important to us — because we are greedy to live — is the future, put a mark on the line that represents today.

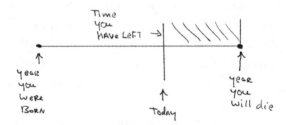

From today to the end of the line is your future. It can be startling to see it so graphically laid before us: It doesn't seem like a lot of time, does it? How many years is it?

Perhaps a knot has formed in your stomach. Thinking about how short the amount of time you have left will do that.

But the feeling will dissolve quickly because we are

addicted to a powerful illusion: "We have time." It is a grand biologically entrenched illusion. It evolved, undoubtedly, so that we would not go insane. It is a hard truth to realize that our lives are short and then we are gone forever. Thus the grand illusion takes over and lulls us back to sleep: *It's okay. You have all the time in the world.*

The first time I did this exercise I was thirty-eight. We'd just had our first daughter, everyone in our family was alive, and time seemed to stretch into a distant and hazy future. No end in sight. Time, being relative, moved slowly. I remember even being bored occasionally. Now, in my sixties, my timeline is sharply focused. Time, my friends, accelerates. I've not been bored, the sitting around with nothing to do kind of bored, in a decade.

I don't have enough time.

To help this sink in, try this tonight as a second part of the exercise. Lie in bed and meditate on your death. Think about how short your life is in contrast to the infinity of time. It's a sobering thought, but it's crucial to understand if you are going to live. Not just exist, but live. There's a difference.

In sum, the first rule of the firefighter's universe is that our lives are short. The time we have remaining is a few decades at the most.

This is just fact. We can believe it to be sobering (and eviscerating) or we can believe it to be liberating. I choose liberating. I choose, since my time on earth is limited, to say "I love you" more. I choose to focus on what is important rather than get mired in stuff that is meaningless. I choose to argue less and appreciate more. I choose to be more compassionate. I choose to spend more time with my family. I choose to be outside more, to enjoy walking our dogs.

All simple things.

You will make your own choices. But let the knowledge that our time here is finite be like a magnifying glass focusing light. Let's not take a second for granted. Let's reflect back every smile. Let's do important stuff.

CHAPTER TWO

THE GLITCH

Everybody has a plan until they get punched in
the mouth.

— MIKE TYSON

Wait! I forgot an important detail of the lifeline exercise.
It's the fine print. I call it the glitch. A story to explain.

We were once paged to a "man down." A typical call. Dozens and dozens of times a year we respond to "man down" 911 calls — usually someone hitchhiking, drunk, stoned, or sleeping.

This time was different. A family out biking. The dad went over a small bump on a bike trail, fell over the handlebars, and broke his neck. Just like that. Just like I was at that time, he was in his thirties. It happened a couple of miles off the road. We knew from our assessment that it was a dire injury. He had no feeling below his belly button. This type of call is a "trauma stat," meaning we need to go fast and alert the trauma team at the hospital. Yet because of the terrain and his injury, it took ten of us almost three hours to slowly carry him out — so careful, so alert not to slip on the rocks.

We would switch positions every few minutes to keep fresh arms and legs carrying the litter. Our patient stared stoically at the sky. We shaded his eyes and gave him sips of water. We, the firefighters, kept looking at one another. We had the sinking feeling that nothing we or the trauma team could do would change the outcome. At the trailhead, we transferred him to our ambulance and began the slow drive over rutted roads to the hospital. Our paramedic that day drew a line on the dad's belly that demarked where he had sensation and where he had none. She wrote the date and the time by the line. She kept testing all the way, praying that it wouldn't change for the worse. Arriving at the hospital, the ambulance driver slumped over the steering wheel, exhausted from avoiding every bump on the dirt roads.

Later that evening, two of us, Dan and I, went to visit the dad in the ICU. The neurologist — who was a friend — confirmed our fears. She told us he had severed his spinal cord at C3. That is the third vertebra in the cervical spine — the beginning of the neck. The information network that flows through our bodies is relatively dispersed, except in our necks. There it turns into a compact and complicated information highway; messages to and from the body run through the cervical spinal canal. An injury there can be a disaster.

"He's a paraplegic now," the doc whispered. "It will take a while for him to come to grips with all this. Don't be long."

She walked away, her long white jacket trailing by her sides.

We went into his room. He was flat on the bed with a big stabilizer holding his head steady. He was staring at the ceiling — there was not much else he could do. He moved his eyes as we came in. Seeing us, he whispered, "Just kill me." Dan and I looked at each other. We talked for a while, and as we left Dan whispered: "This sucks."

A beautiful day. Vacation. A lovely family. "Good people." Then this.

Maybe it was because we were all mostly new to first responding, or we could so easily see ourselves in him and his family, but this call got to us. The next day at lunch, the treating paramedic said it best: "I always thought that karma was a real thing. If you're good in the world, good things happen to you…"

Her voice trailed off.

The glitch simply is this: We can have plans, we can have our lifeline taped to our bathroom mirror, we can be good people, anxious people, or cautious people. But the fact is, stuff happens. That's the glitch. Out of the blue, in the space of one day, everything can change.

A car sails into yours. A home burns down. A child comes home defeated. A niece becomes an addict. You lose your job. The doctor calls with a cancer diagnosis. You tumble off a bicycle.

Firefighting is a doctorate in the glitch, in the science of Stuff Happens. It is what we do, see, and learn each time there is a 911 call.

The cliché is that being a firefighter (or any first responder) toughens your skin, gives you a protective layer of scar tissue. I think it's the opposite. Being a firefighter takes a layer of skin off, peels the onion, makes you more aware of the glitch, of the fact that anything can happen on any given day and send your lifeline careening in an entirely new direction.

Now, you can consider this dark or tragic. I prefer to think of it as "just how it is." It's how the universe works, one of the rules.

How we respond to the fact that life has glitches is up to us.

It seems to me — to be binary for a moment — that we have two choices. If we understand that life is short and unpredictable, we can sink into despair and nihilism, thinking that there is no meaning here and we can never find joy. That, to me, is lazy thinking or maybe the phase one goes through during sophomore year of college. The other option is to accept the glitch, accept uncertainty, and get on with living. Not just waiting around until we die or until the glitch gets us, but get on with living.

Being a firefighter, understanding and accepting uncertainty in our bones, brings all this into focus. Little things matter more. I am amazed by my kids' laughter, my wife's touch.

Of course, because I am often witness to the unplanned, to the surprises in the night, sometimes the glitch leaves me thunderstruck.

A few years ago, a blizzard shut down the interstate in our fire district. The roads were so treacherous that state police cars were positioned to block anyone from driving over a nearby mountain pass. Late that night my pager went off, but it was hard to understand what the dispatcher was saying. I assumed, because of the weather, that the 911 call was for a car crash. I got up, put on the warmest clothes I could find, and went out the door. Because the call was near our home, I was first on the scene. A little pickup truck was on the side of the road. It didn't look damaged. But as I got out of my truck,

I heard the dispatcher clearly say that this was an emergency birth, that a woman was in labor in the back seat.

Talk about a glitch in a birth plan: a blizzard, roads closed, going into labor.

I got to the truck, opened the door, and heard that baby cry. I remember thinking it was the most wonderful sound I'd ever experienced. The father, a nurse, had already delivered the baby, who was fine. Our ambulance appeared through the snow and mist. We wrapped mom and baby up, got them in the ambulance, and with a police escort, they headed to the hospital.

Here is the lesson. We can hold both of these thoughts at the same time: Life is short and there's the glitch. And yet, always there is the cry of a newborn. That lusty wail that launches a new timeline is a sound that defies all logic; it is the cry "I am" to the dark universe.

Thunderstruck.

CHAPTER THREE

GOD, CHAOS,
AND FIREFIGHTERS

Impermanence is life's only promise to us, and she
keeps it with ruthless impeccability.

— JENNIFER WELWOOD, "The Dakini Speaks"

In explaining the firefighter universe, I feel it's important to
note that firefighters are not philosophers. We are a practical bunch. Nor are we priests, rabbis, or Zen masters. Yet we
operate in a part of the universe where we often come face to
face with essential philosophical and spiritual questions, like,
Why did this happen?

Sometimes the answer is simple.

The page went out, "Structure fire, 15 Leaping Powder
Road." I was close by, so I drove to the scene. There was no
smoke, no flames, just a woman waving me down.

I reported what I saw on the radio and got out of my
car. The woman apologetically told me the fire was out, but I
could come in and check it out if I wanted.

I followed her into her jeweler's studio. There was a pile
of burnt and wet papers on her studio table.

She looked at me and shrugged sheepishly. "I left my

jeweler's magnifying lens focused on the table." She pointed to it and then to the table. "The sun shone through the lens and set the papers on fire! I put it out and then called 911. I guess I kinda panicked. Why does stuff like this always happen to me?"

The answer to her question is physics. Sunlight shining through a lens creates enough heat to ignite paper. Full stop. No more inquiry needed.

For most of our calls, the why behind them can be answered the same way: physics, chemistry, biology, often mixed in with bad choices.

But sometimes the question comes at you hard.

Once at a memorial service after a particularly tragic crash, a mom — whose daughter was a friend of the victims — came up to me, grabbed me by the shoulders, and cried, "How could this happen?"

She wasn't looking for the "physics" answer. Instead, her orderly, logical universe had been dealt a mortal blow, had been sundered. She wanted real answers to the question why.

It is an existential question, one that no fire academy prepares you for, so firefighters are left — like all of us — to figure it out for ourselves.

When I was six, my sister died of leukemia. Mortal blow, world sundered. The priest had a ready answer to the question why. To him, it was simple: "It was God's will."

That answer never satisfied. Of course, it brings up other unanswerable questions. Becoming a firefighter and seeing what we see, that answer makes less sense now than it ever did.

We're still continuously faced with the question why.

As humans, we seem to have this deep explanatory need, this desire to ask and answer that question.

Were I a philosopher, I would start by eliminating options. First, as the Stoics wrote in the third century BC, it isn't the gods getting revenge. They mused that the gods are neutral. I see no lightning bolts flashing out of the sky striking down the wicked.

Nor do I particularly believe in karma, at least not the kind limited to one lifetime. Bad things happen across the board, to the young, the old, the good, the guilty, the doubters, the ambitious, the lazy, and the believers. The universe turns a blind eye to all.

Once we transported two elderly women who were hit by a drunk driver. They were both in critical condition in the hospital. The two drunks — whom we also transported — had minor injuries and were laughing and enjoying themselves in the ER. Ask any firefighter how many times they've seen that drama play out. See it enough times, and it complicates your catechism.

This means, as you already know, that I eliminate "big G" God as a direct and proximate cause. I see no saints being magically protected either.

Fourteen billion years ago, the big bang happened, the laws of physics were launched, and they seem to be running the show. How that all came into being or what happened before… Please, I'm a firefighter, I have no idea.

In the debate between God and physics, I choose physics.

An important joke:

Sven was walking along a fjord in Norway. He slipped and fell off the cliff and barely missed falling to his death by grabbing a ledge. Now he was trapped: ten feet from the top and one hundred feet from the bottom.

Sven called out, "Help! Is there anyone up there!?"

Nothing.

He called again in desperation, and a booming voice answered, "Sven, this is God. Trust me. Let go of the ledge and fall. You shall not be injured."

Sven thought for a moment and called out again, "Is there anyone else up there?"

It's not that Sven didn't believe in God. But he also believed in the rules of the universe, in physics.

God is mysterious. The rules of the universe — as far as firefighters see them play out — are reasonably clear. A jeweler's magnifying glass focusing the sun on paper will start a fire. A drunk taking a corner too fast in a car will roll over. A man lets go of the cliff, he will fall.

What then is the answer?

Stop and listen to the deeper drumbeat of the universe. If we do this, we learn that the answer to the question of why the drunk lived, why the family was killed, is that we live in a chaotic universe.

The rules of physics dictate that chaos exists. Now, Newton and Einstein might see beauty and order in the cosmos, but I think if you look at it from the perspective of a clever ape, it seems chaotic. In the big picture, we live on this whirling little green-and-blue planet on the outskirts of a spinning galaxy among comets and meteors (that occasionally smash into us, rendering mass extinctions), exploding stars, black holes, and colliding galaxies. All of this exists in a rapidly expanding universe that may be a bubble in a sea of universes. On the microscopic level, we are in an evolutionary battle for our lives against microbes and disease.

Chaos.

Charles Darwin, it is said, turned away from God (at least

partially) because he couldn't accept that a beneficent God would create such a monster as the parasitic wasp, which lays its eggs inside a living caterpillar. Then, the larvae of the wasp eat the caterpillar from the inside out while it still lives.

In the same way, as a firefighter, it is hard for me to accept the universe as orderly or that there is a grand plan. We see too many lifelines spiraling out of control. Thus I have accepted as fact that physics rules and "chaos" is often the answer to our perennial question. "Stuff happens" is often the answer. Full stop. Every time the pager wails in the middle of the night is testament to this.

But it befuddles me. I don't think it is right to answer a crying mom who asks, "How could this happen?" with the glib answer, "Because stuff happens." Or for that matter, "Because God willed it."

So instead, often awkwardly, I just say, "I'm so sorry. What can I do to help?"

Maybe that is the answer. In a chaotic universe, all we have is one another. To help create love and caring, to help make meaning of our existence, we have one another.

CHAPTER FOUR

SO, DEATH

how do you like your blue-eyed boy / Mister Death

— E.E. CUMMINGS, "Buffalo Bill's"

Jürgen was driving that night. It was 4 AM, and we were on our way back to the station from the hospital. Jürgen was the only anarchist-atheist-socialist firefighter I've ever known, and he was a dedicated firefighter. However, I rarely let him drive. He was an insane German driver and always thought he was on the autobahn. I was holding on to the door handles with a death grip. The morning was primordially dark. Then — taking our breath away — the sky suddenly turned bright and brilliant green. It was day for seconds. A meteor flashed overhead to the horizon and then disappeared. The dark closed over us again. We didn't even have time to say, "What the hell was that?" before it was gone.

Clearly, the meteor was a signal to Jürgen — who was philosophical by nature and could yak your ears off — to talk about more significant things. We were quiet for a moment contemplating what had just happened. Then Jürgen said, "You know why I became a firefighter? It's because I wanted to bring death and suffering into my life. Three generations ago everyone knew how to deliver a baby and embalm their parents. Everyone experienced death regularly. I needed to bring death into my life so that I could understand" — terrifying me, he took both hands off the steering wheel and stretched his arms out wide — "what this is all about."

Most firefighters are not as naturally pensive as Jürgen. He was, after all, German. His central point — that to truly understand the gift of life, we need to be familiar with death — rings true. It's death that gives life meaning. That we will die gives life its sweetness. That others suffer and die makes it the greatest sin to waste our lives or take them for granted.

By the nature of the work, firefighters invite death into their lives. They become accustomed to it with all its variations. From bedrooms to streets to emergency rooms, death and dying are part and parcel of every day. We become objective about dying.

It took me a while to accept the objectification of death. I was raised in a family that never brought the subject up and in a society that is still in denial about death in general.

It was always a shocking conversation whenever the topic was broached.

When I was twenty-two, I once dated another dancer from Winnipeg. On our first date, after only one glass of wine, she blurted out, "Why do we have to die?" Then she burst into tears.

I had to think hard about going out with her again, but it was a confusing time of my life, and she was beautiful and intense, so I did.

But in that moment, I didn't understand the question. Who's going to die? We're going to live forever!

That was the last conversation I had about death and dying until I became a firefighter.

Then, everything changed. Death became familiar.

A Good First Death

Laurie and I had been active members for just shy of four months. It was a July day in New Mexico, which meant thunderstorms, when the 911 page came in.

REEEE! "Hondo, respond to Pecos, Highway 63. Possible cardiac arrest. Lightning strike."

Pecos was thirty miles away. It might as well have been three million miles for someone in cardiac arrest. It would take forty minutes to get there. Witnesses estimated that the patient had been down for at least fifteen minutes.

When Laurie and the rest of the crew arrived on the scene, the patient, a middle-aged Hispanic man, was already covered head to toe with a sheet.

Laurie felt to confirm that there was no pulse. She noticed that he was a waxen white color. He was wearing a baseball hat, and his head was still smoking from the lightning strike. One of the other medics noted that he was smoking from both ends: his shoes had been blown off and his feet were smoking.

The crew completed their paperwork, left the body to the state police, jumped back in the rig, and headed home.

That night Laurie mused, "On the way back, Dan said that I was lucky. This had been pretty good for a first death. There was no real trauma. It was an adult. There was nothing we could do. All in all, he thought I was lucky."

There is a lot of subtext here. First, there is the simple

matter-of-factness about death, the familiarity with it. Firefighters learn they can be saddened by it, but death doesn't surprise.

Instead, death is ubiquitous. Once, while I was standing in our kitchen, I watched a sharp-shinned hawk swoop down out of a tree close to our house and catch a sparrow at our feeder. She held that sparrow to the ground until it died. It took minutes for the sparrow's life to pass. I was mesmerized. Then the hawk flew off with its prey.

Death is all around us, all the time. Yet we wear blinders; we are good at not seeing, not experiencing death. As a result, we are unaccustomed to it, this natural part of our world.

Second, Dan's comment carried an implicit warning. Although this was a good first death, other deaths are heart-wrenching. Our task as firefighters is to be ready to handle those because it is our job. It is our job to deal with the dying and the dead.

The Outer Circle

We learn how to deal with death over time, over a few dozen deaths. It sounds coldhearted, but it isn't. It is self-preservation.

In the fire department, we use outer and inner circles when we are dealing with a bad car crash. The outer circle is where we stand if we are not actively involved in the call. We wait to be needed, watching and just being ready. In the inner circle, we're close to or inside a crushed car. There, in the inner circle, you're 100 percent focused and acutely aware of what is going on. An inner-circle medic can be inside the car treating an entangled patient while the rest of the crew cuts the car apart. It can be an intimate experience.

I think of deaths in the same way. For most deaths, firefighters stand in the outer circle. We don't know the person; we are removed from the situation. The man struck by lightning was an outer-circle death. We do our jobs, but they are deaths we usually walk away from knowing that we did everything we could. In the outer circle, we are clinical, steps removed from the dying. We're detached but hardworking. We're devoted but at a distance.

It's easier to explain death and dying from the perspective of that outer circle.

Death exists on a sliding scale. There is clinical death when the heart stops beating. There is biological death when organs — heart, kidneys — are deprived of oxygen and begin to fail. Then there is brain death when the neurons in the brain give up the ghost. Then it's over. Lights out.

In the movie *The Princess Bride*, Miracle Max describes this best: "It just so happens that your friend here is only *mostly* dead. There's a big difference between mostly dead and all dead. Mostly dead is slightly alive. With all dead, well, with all dead there's usually only one thing you can do. Go through his clothes and look for loose change."

In the field, in our service, given the above, we have rules about who can declare someone "all dead." Firefighters can't. EMTs can't. Only paramedics — who are more highly trained than EMTs — can declare someone dead. There are exceptions that we call the obviously dead, but most of the time death has to be confirmed by a paramedic.

The Inner Circle

On my first cardiac arrest, there were no paramedics. I had beaten our ambulance up the wintery road and gotten to the home first. It was night, the house was lit up, but there was no one to meet us. I went in, called out, found nothing. I went to the back patio, and there was our patient on his back, arms akimbo on the stone walkway. He was dusted with snow. He had dropped to the ground, just like that. He was young, in his fifties. I knelt down, felt for a pulse; there was none, and he wasn't breathing.

I was consumed by the desire to do the right thing. I started CPR and yelled out for help. Right then, a woman came running around the corner in the snow wearing a bathrobe and Sorel boots — it turned out she was his wife, and she'd been looking for us — and she let out a shriek, "Save him, please God, save him."

In EMT class, we are taught that you can't be distracted by bystanders, that you have to focus on the work. But her agony unnerved me.

She dropped to her knees in the snow and cried behind me, "Please save him! He's going to be all right — you'll save him…" Her voice trailed off. I focused on counting compressions on his chest.

After an eternity, I heard other voices; it was the crew from our ambulance. They knelt down, and together we began working a basic code. We continued compressions, stripped his pajamas off, attached the pads for the defibrillator, and got an airway and oxygen started.

We tried to shock him, but the defib voice, cold and calm, said, "No shock advised." That meant to us that our patient did not have a shockable rhythm, and we didn't have the drugs or skills to do anything but continue CPR.

Alan, one of the other EMTs, looked at me and shook his head, but said, "Let's get him in the ambulance and go."

And we did, but only because we had a tacit agreement that we weren't going to stop treating the patient in front of his wife. We were going to take him to the hospital — work him all the way — and let the nurses and the docs declare him dead.

As we left, his wife was still on her knees being comforted by a neighbor. But she knew she'd lost her husband and she was inconsolable.

That is an inner-circle moment. Most of us will experience death in that kind of moment, and there is nothing that prepares you for it. An elderly patient once told me that you can't really understand or accept death until someone close to you dies and that, she insisted, includes firefighters.

Growing Up

The thesis of this chapter is simple: When we accept death at an emotional level, our death, the death of our loved ones, it can be freeing. "Freeing" doesn't mean without pain or suffering. Rather, there are so many shackles that bind us; the need to conform, the desire for "things," anger and impatience. When we understand that this is it, our one little life bounded by death, those shackles lose their power. When we look at someone we love and realize they have their own lifeline and they will die, it's easier to let go of anger. When we understand and accept death, life becomes more vivid in all its aspects.

The genesis of that late-night conversation between Jürgen and me driving home in the ambulance — other than the meteor — was that we had lost another patient, and we were yet again coming to grips with death. It was one more marker in the process of us growing up as firefighters and as human beings.

Yet that meteor lighting up the skies is a perfect metaphor for the firefighter universe. We see a lot of darkness, but every once in a while, at four in the morning when the world is asleep, we get the brilliance of green-white-blue light that illuminates the world for us to see.

CHAPTER FIVE

COWBOY KICKED BY DEAD COW

Tragedy is when I cut my finger. Comedy is when
you fall into an open sewer and die.

— MEL BROOKS

REEEE! "Hondo, respond to I-25 mile marker 286. Man kicked by dead cow. Possible broken leg…"

Our chatter on the radio as we headed out was, "Huh? Really?"

Pulling up on the scene, we found several state police cars and a big tractor trailer that had apparently overturned a few hours before. It was a bizarre scene. There were cows grazing in the median and wandering off into fields alongside the road. Dead cows were also lying on the highway.

A couple of workers were loading carcasses into pickup trucks with a front-end loader. We grabbed our medical bags and walked over to the center of the scene. An officer saw us and pointed to a cowboy sitting on the ground, grimacing in pain.

Completely matter-of-fact, the officer told us what had happened. The truck was hauling cattle to Colorado when it overturned. Quite a few cows had been killed. It took a while to figure out who to call and how to remove the living as well as the dead cattle from the trailer. After all the living cows had been shooed out, a couple of workers had gone into the trailer to haul out the dead ones — there's a fun job.

It had been a few hours. It was hot, and rigor mortis had begun to set in. Two of the workers were yanking a cow off another dead one when the dead cow's stiff leg snapped back and kicked one of the workers.

Raised eyebrows and questioning looks met the state police officer. That was the story, and the officer played it straight, cowboy straight, state police officer straight. He didn't even smile or blink. He walked us over to the worker. Yep, visible ankle fracture.

I asked the cowboy if it hurt. He just gritted his teeth and mumbled, "Little bit."

Another medic casually leaned back and looked into the trailer. She turned back to the crew and whispered, "It wasn't a dead cow. It was a zombie cow that kicked him. That cow knew exactly what she was doing."

None of us said a word. We splinted his ankle while the treating EMT asked the standard questions, although she left out any mention of possible zombie-mad-cow-disease infection. We loaded him into our ambulance and wove our way through the surviving cattle that were obliviously grazing on the median grass.

I was driving, and I listened to the medic in the back make her report to the hospital: "St. Vincent's Hospital, Hondo is transporting a twenty-four-year-old male to your ER. Patient reports he was kicked by a dead cow. He has a possible right ankle fracture. Patient is alert with stable vitals. Our ETA is ten minutes."

There was a pause. A nurse's voice finally came back and politely asked, "Hondo, could you repeat?"

"Yep," the medic replied. "Twenty-four-year-old male. Kicked by dead cow. Ankle fracture. Ten minutes out."

Another pause. A male voice came on. "Did you say cow or dead cow?"

"Dead cow. Fractured ankle. Seven minutes out."

Silence. Then, "Okay. We'll see you in a few. St. Vincent's out."

It is not possible to survive mentally intact as a firefighter without a deep and dark sense of humor.

It isn't that firefighters are naturally funny, although humor is highly regarded. Firefighters simply report what they see, and what they see is often darkly comedic.

"The code" instructs that we keep our humor inside the firehouse, between firefighters, because you have to be grounded in tragedy. Occasionally it slips out in public conversation, and a story that we think of as hilarious is met with stunned silence. Experiencing a few of those moments teaches you to only speak to the brother- and sisterhood.

Humor is an antonym of suffering. It is the ability to see the comedic, sometimes in the darkest of times, that allows you to get up and go on the next call, and the next. Firefighter humor isn't necessarily laugh-out-loud funny — although there is plenty of that — rather it evokes the abiding sense of the craziness that we come across.

Once we had a patient who shot himself in the forehead with a .22-caliber handgun. He was high on cocaine and thought he was invincible. Fortunately for him, the bullet did not penetrate his skull, but it avulsed his scalp, tearing open the skin from his forehead to the crown of his head. We transported him — the three of us in the back marveling at his luck. We forever called him "Bang-in-the-head."

Two decades later, I ran into him at a gas station. A guy at the next pump smiled at me and asked me how I was doing. He mentioned that he couldn't believe how expensive gas was. He smiled again and limped toward the store to pay. I took a closer look. He was in his forties, had a cane, his face drooped on one side. He had a vertical scar that ran from his nose up past his hairline. I realized after a second that I recognized him. I said, "Hey, I remember you. We transported you about fifteen years ago, for a gunshot wound."

He looked at the fire department license plate, smiled crookedly at me again, and said, "Yeah, yeah, that was me. Dude, I was way fucked up. I didn't get better for a long time."

He stepped closer and whispered conspiratorially, "I got married after that, and I was making seven hundred and fifty dollars cash every week. I was giving my wife two hundred dollars a week, and I spent the rest on three grams of coke, twelve hits of acid, and a case of beer. I kept doing that until one night I freaked out and tried to shoot myself again with a 12-gauge. But my wife called the state police, and they came and tackled me before I could do it. Yeah…"

He paused, thinking.

"I'm better now." He smiled and walked off.

Another time we responded to a "female, unconscious, possibly drunk." We arrived at a large party outside on the street. People were surrounding a young woman who had apparently passed out. They let us through, and I went up to our patient, gently nudging her to see if I could wake her up. She bolted upright, swung at me as hard as she could, punched me in the jaw before I could react, threw up (projectile!), and then collapsed back in her vomit. I survived. Hilarity among the partiers ensued.

On a September Saturday, we were paged to a motorcycle crash about twenty miles from our station. Driving past the scene, we could see the motorcycle in the ditch. It was a mangled wreck on the two-lane asphalt road that headed toward the town of Galisteo. This road was high-speed motorcycle heaven unless you missed a turn or hit a rabbit.

Sam, our paramedic for the day, gave instructions, "Call for Life Flight. Get the airway bag, spineboard, and oxygen."

Opening the passenger door of the ambulance, he got out. "Let's see what we got!" Three of us walked over to a crowd of people, and as they parted, Sam yelled, "Jesus Christ! What the fuck are you doing?"

Sam was one of our more "ramped up" paramedics.

He was addressing a tall woman with long flowing blonde hair, a flowery dress, and sandals. She was sitting cross-legged with the apparent patient, who had what looked to be a significant head injury. Blood covered his face, and there was a dark slick of blood on the right side of his head. Obviously, no helmet. From the looks of the motorcycle, it was a high-speed crash. The woman had the rider's head cradled in her lap, and she was rocking him gently.

"Um," she replied, a little taken aback. "Like, he's hurt. He's hurt really bad. I chanted for him. I thought if I rocked him and gave him some Rescue Remedy, it would help."

Sam, never an easy-going paramedic, really went ballistic.

"You moved him! What if his neck is broken, did you think about that?"

"His neck?" She started to get weepy. "Dude, ah, like he was bleeding from his head. He needed a friend. I could sense that his aura needed healing."

She ran her hands over his body and head. "I'm not touching him. I'm just rebuilding his energy field."

Sam was dumbstruck. "Fuck, and you're giving him Rescue Remedy? To a head injury? Jesus!"

Rescue Remedy is a New Age herbal medicine mixed with water and brandy.

Our hippie Good Samaritan held up the bottle for Sam to see, her voice rising, "It says right on the label: Good for trauma. Will calm the patient. Give liberally."

Standing there, we were all thinking the same thing: This guy was barely conscious and about to lose control of his airway. Pouring fluids down it could not only occlude it but it might make him vomit. Also, just what every head-injured person needs: alcohol!

We convinced Sam to walk away and not strangle her. We packaged the biker and loaded him on the helicopter. Hippie-girl, true to her colors, arms over her head, yelled, "Blessed be!" as the chopper took off and flew to Albuquerque.

Once we were paged to a "bleeding call." On arrival, we found a thirty-seven-year-old guy who had just had rectal surgery. Somehow, he had reopened the incision and was bleeding profusely. The blood was bright red and spurting, so we knew it was an arterial bleed, which we had to stop quickly. With gloves on, I grabbed a big abdominal pad and pushed it up between the guy's legs and applied pressure. While I was doing this, a couple of the other medics started IVs.

Dan went out to the ambulance to call the ER and let them know what we had.

The bleeding was so bad I used another abdominal pad, and an EMT started asking the patient questions, when all of a sudden her eyes went wide. I turned to look, and it was Dan, now completely covered in a white Tyvek suit, hood, booties, goggles, and mask.

He bent down and whispered through his mask, "The ER knows this guy." He nodded toward the patient. "They ordered us to use *full protection*."

I'm sure my eyes showed a hint of panic...I was stuck holding pressure with my arm between our patient's legs.

"Shit," I muttered.

The hospital didn't supply any details. They had to protect patient confidentiality. Thus our imaginations ran wild as we carefully loaded the man onto the gurney — and he was friendly and helpful the entire time, which was notable, considering where my arm was, since I had to maintain pressure on the wound. In the ambulance, I knelt at the end of the gurney trying to avoid eye contact with the guy and praying that there were no holes in my gloves. We drove slowly out of the driveway and then hit the lights and sirens to the hospital — not because this was a real emergency, but because I was pleading for the driver to hurry so that I could get my hand out of there, take off all my clothes, and shower.

These calls weave themselves into the fabric of first responding and confirm that even in our small district, dark comedy rules.

I think the question is, What do we do when we smash up against the reality of life, which is crazy, unpredictable, and rarely works out the way we plan? Our first reaction may be to double down on orderliness, stick to our schedule, ignore the mess.

Another path is to embrace the mess, to become poets of the absurd, to let go of order, to laugh at it. Like having a baby for the first time: You learn to accept the toys, changing tables, diapers, no sleep, and mess that comes with children.

The middle way is to accept a little of both. Where and when necessary, when possible, impose order, do the work, clean the house. But know it won't last, see the absurdity. When the guy with the crossbow arrow through his neck tells you to be careful, it is okay to smile while still treating the patient with the utmost care and professionalism. Yes, of course, we will be careful, but treating a guy with an arrow through his neck is not something you see every day.

The middle way asks us to try while not taking ourselves or the messiness of life too seriously.

Albert Camus, the French existentialist — and poet of the absurd — commented on the myth of Sisyphus that we are all doomed to continue to push that rock up the mountain only to have it roll back again and have to start over. He warned that even though the task is absurd, we have to defiantly find meaning in the task. As a firefighter, I would add (humbly), after thousands of calls both tragic and comic, that we also need to continually find humor in the absurd if we are to survive mentally intact.

"Hondo, respond to 15 Seton Village Road. Man with cockroach in his ear."

Five minutes later: "Hondo, cancel the call, the cockroach crawled out."

CHAPTER SIX

RITES OF PASSAGE

> Like all explorers, we are drawn to discover what's
> waiting out there without knowing yet if we have
> the courage to face it.
>
> — PEMA CHÖDRÖN, *When Things Fall Apart*

All firefighters find themselves on their own unique journey through the vocation. Yet there are common way-
points, rivers that are crossed, as you mature as a firefighter.

If you are lucky — as Laurie and I were — you get a few
simple calls under your belt early: a car fire, a lightning strike.
These teach you how to act as a firefighter.

Our first few years were perfect in that regard. Contrary
to the warnings we were given, being a firefighter-EMT was a
stress reducer. The pager would go off, we'd get out of meet-
ings, and for a few minutes or hours, we could leave the stress
of work and our normal lives and focus on someone else. We
were working with great people, we were building friendships,
and it seemed exciting.

By our second year, we also believed that we understood
firefighting. We thought we were hardened. (You make plans

and the universe laughs.) We'd had a few more deaths, lots of drunk drivers, a couple of overdoses, and about a dozen fires.

But there was a rite of passage still to be navigated. It didn't end in a badge or a promotion ceremony. It was when the universe plays its true hand and asks if you're ready.

That happened for me on a July evening in the middle of monsoon season in Santa Fe. It was my third year.

The page went out, "Motor vehicle crash, extrication required, Galisteo River." I hopped in my truck and drove to the end of our road, sliding in the slick mud, and stopped, waiting, windshield wipers on high. Going south toward that part of the region, department procedure was to pick me up on the way. It was raining so hard that I couldn't see more than a half mile. Finally, our old green rescue truck, its strobe lights glittering in the downpour, pulled up, and I jumped in the back with two other firefighters.

We drove down the long curving road that cut through the volcanic escarpments into the Galisteo Basin. The rain was coming down so hard that as it bounced off the road, it created a curtain of water.

Dispatch came over the radio, "Responding units, no law enforcement available. The storm has flooded out roads all over the county. State police is coming from up north. ETA forty minutes."

It was twilight when we arrived on the scene. The rain was still hard and driving. Low clouds scudded across the basin with thunder and streaks of lightning to the south.

We got out of the truck. A passerby got out of his car and ran toward us.

"I was behind 'em," he said. "The bridge is washed out by the river. They didn't see it. They flew off the road and slammed into the bank on the other side! There's a bunch of kids in the car! We couldn't get them out. You gotta do something before the river takes the car!"

Our captain, Lindsey, and I walked over to the bank, buckling our gear. My heart rate was going up.

Lindsey got on his handheld radio and announced to all the incoming units, "I have one vehicle in the water. Possible multiple patients. Extrication needed."

He pointed at me. "You got triage. Let's get them out as quick as we can."

The car was in fast-moving water about two feet deep. As I waded into the river, staying balanced was hard. I made it to the back door. It was jammed shut by the pressure of the current. A woman in the back seat was leaning against the front seat. I pounded on the window. Nothing.

Another firefighter said, "Wait a minute!" He reached into his pocket and brought out a window punch. Putting it against the back window, he pulled the trigger and the window shattered.

We brushed away the broken glass. I reached in and touched her shoulder.

"Hey, ma'am! Are you okay?" I yelled over the sound of rushing water and pounding rain.

I dropped to my knees in the water so that I could get closer to her.

"Can you hear me?" I asked again.

The car lurched a bit in the current. From above I heard Lindsey shout, "Be careful. Watch the car if it starts to go!"

The woman opened her eyes, turned her head, and looked at me, "I'm fine, I'm okay. Please, just get my kids out. Please!"

I stood up. Another EMT on the downstream side of the

car yelled at me. "I've got three patients. Two kids and the dad. All minor injuries but they're cold! All conscious. Dad's bleeding on the back of his head, but he's talking to me."

I relayed the information to Lindsey.

"Okay. Let's get them out first! Be careful," he yelled back over pounding rain.

The other two firefighters nodded. I knelt back in the river, so I could talk to "mom" and begin an assessment.

"Get the kids out!" she insisted, "I'm fine!"

"Look," I said and pointed to the other side of the car.

They were pulling both kids out through the window. "They're getting the kids out now. We're going to put them in an ambulance, dry them off, get 'em warm, and they'll be fine."

I could feel myself relaxing.

This is how it goes, I thought, *a couple minutes of chaos and then everything falls into place.*

I spoke again to the mom, "Your husband is next, all right?"

She nodded.

"He's got a cut on his head, and he's freezing. We have to pry his door open. But the worst is over! Then we'll open your door with our tools. But we gotcha."

The mom asked me again, "Are the kids okay? Tell me the truth!"

"They're fine," I repeated. "It's going to be okay."

I saw the dad being helped up the slope. He was wet and muddy but walking. In order to open the mom's door, three firefighters lugged our portable hydraulic spread across the river to the other side, closer to the car. They started it up, unwound the lines, and walked the tool down.

I squeezed her hand. "We'll have you out in a minute."

She nodded. She looked a little pale, tired but relieved.

She leaned back in her seat. She had a laceration on her forehead.

"Does that hurt?" I asked.

"What?" she replied slowly. "Does what hurt?"

"Your head, you have a cut on your forehead."

"I do?" she asked. She slowly put her hand up to her head. Pulling her hand away, she saw the blood.

"Huh, I don't feel anything."

A little knot formed in my stomach.

The firefighter behind me tapped me on the shoulder. "Back off for a minute. We'll pull the door away."

I pulled the board and the now-soaking blanket away and got off my knees. The extrication team slid in, popped the door from the frame, and tossed it into the river.

I got back on my knees by the woman.

"Do you know what day it is?" I asked.

"Um," she paused and then said, "I think it's Tuesday, right?"

It was Friday.

The knot in my stomach tightened. But I said to myself, *She hit her head on the seat in front of her. Probably just a concussion.*

We got her packaged. Her head was still bleeding. I put a trauma pad on her scalp and shielded her eyes from the rain with my hand.

She looked up at me. She looked worn.

"Kids are, um, okay, right?" she asked me again, reaching for my hand.

I nodded, "Yep. They're fine. Let's take care of you now."

Six of us slowly carried her on the backboard out of the river, up the slope, and into the ambulance.

Lindsey walked over to me. "We called for a helicopter because of her head injury, just to be safe."

I nodded. I started to dry her off so that she wouldn't get hypothermic.

She retook my hand. "The kids, the kids are okay, right?"

"Yep, they're fine," I said. "They are on the way to the hospital with their dad. They're not hurt, just a precaution."

The side door opened. A gust of wind and rain blew through. Lindsey stuck his head in. "Look, the helicopter can't land. The weather sucks. We need to go to Santa Fe and St. Vincent's, okay?"

I nodded. "Let's just get going."

Lindsey answered, "We've got a paramedic from Torrance County. He's gonna jump in with you."

I nodded, relieved. I reached over the gurney, grabbed an oxygen mask, and gently placed it on the mom's face.

The side door opened again, and the paramedic jumped in.

"What do we got?" he asked.

I quickly briefed him as he looked at our patient.

"Let's do a full assessment, okay? Get her clothes off and do a head-to-toe. I'll get her vitals."

"Okay," I nodded.

I looked at her. She seemed a bit quieter than before. She smiled wanly.

I examined her. Her forehead was lacerated, and her hair was wet and caked with blood. The back of her neck seemed fine, no pain or visible deformities. I opened her shirt and checked her shoulders: fine. Chest: fine. It was too noisy to listen to lung sounds, but her chest rise seemed regular and symmetrical. I palpated her belly, starting with the upper half. The upper quadrants seemed normal. When I pressed down, she didn't react in pain. But when I pushed down the lower left part of her belly, she winced a bit.

Then I noticed a small line of bruising below her belly button. It crossed her entire abdomen as if it was painted on.

Probably, I thought, *just bruising from her seat belt.*

"Were you wearing a seat belt?" I asked her to confirm my suspicion.

She didn't answer right away. Then she looked at me. "What?"

Before I could ask again, the paramedic swore under his breath.

"Fuck! This can't be right!"

He looked hard at me and whispered, "We gotta go. Her BP is only eighty over forty, pulse is one-thirty."

I looked at him, not understanding. She had a head injury, right? Her blood pressure should be normal, maybe a little high.

He just repeated, "We gotta go!"

"Um, okay. I'll get us going."

I stuck my head out the door. It was still pouring rain. "Lindsey! We have to go! Right now!"

Lindsey shook his head. "We talked to St. Vincent's. They said not to come. They're backed up. You need to go to Albuquerque."

Then, the mother, I didn't even know her name, looked at me one more time and closed her eyes. I bent down and said, "Hey, Mom!" Nothing. I rubbed her sternum. I rubbed it again, urgently. Nothing.

"Hey, Mom," I yelled, "Wake up."

"Jesus," the paramedic whispered again under his breath as he felt for a carotid pulse.

I glanced down at her belly. The small line of bruising had grown. The area between her belly button and pelvis was black and blue.

"No pulse!" the paramedic yelled.

"That can't be," I said, "she was just talking to me…"

"Start CPR!" he yelled again as he turned to get the defibrillator off the shelf.

I started compressions. There were just two of us. The paramedic was working furiously: attaching the pads, yelling at me to stop compressions.

The paramedic hit the analyze button on the defibrillator, and that disembodied voice said, "Shock advised." He hit the shock button; the defibrillator charged and delivered its load of electricity. She jerked spasmodically.

"Analyzing," the voice called out. "No shock advised; continue patient care."

The paramedic swore, "Jesus fucking Christ!"

He nodded at me, and I continued compressions.

I checked for a carotid pulse. I noticed my hands were shaking. There was nothing.

We worked furiously for a few more minutes. The paramedic gave her epinephrine through the endotracheal tube. Then again. And a third time. Nothing changed. I stopped CPR and felt again for a pulse. Nothing. She wasn't breathing.

Then the defibrillator screen confirmed what we knew. Asystole. We'd lost her. She was dead.

"Fuck," the paramedic whispered to himself. He sat down and put his hands over his face. He had jumped into our rig to help with a head laceration and possible concussion.

There was nothing we could do. Her husband and kids

were already on the way to St. Vincent's ER. They were all minor injuries, so the ER was accepting. They would be waiting for the mom to show up. After all, I had yelled to them that she was going to be right behind them.

Lindsey opened the door, wondering why we were still there, and saw our mom, arms outstretched, eyes staring blankly into space, the detritus of a cardiac code — IV tubing, sharps containers with needles, defibrillator pads — spread throughout the ambulance.

"Shit," Lindsey finally said. "Goddamnit."

"She was gone, man," the paramedic said to me. "There was nothing we could do. Nothing."

He shook his head. "Sorry," he whispered.

He jumped out of our rig and headed back to his truck.

Lindsey was quiet for a moment. The rain pounded on the roof of the ambulance.

"Look," Lindsey said, "why don't I grab someone else to ride in with her. We need to take her into the morgue — I mean the hospital."

"No, I got it. I'll do it."

I sat on the bench seat next to her. I put my hand on her shoulder. I stared at the back window.

There's a big clock in the back of our ambulance. When we left the river and the wrecked car, it was 8:14. We drove up out of the basin. The storm was breaking up; the moon was rising over the volcanic dikes, creating a dark and dramatic landscape. We rose to the plains outside of Santa Fe.

The next time I looked at the clock, we were at the hospital. It was 9:24. I wrote that down: "Arrived at hospital, 9:24 PM. Body turned over to morgue staff. Hondo back in service, 9:50 PM."

We learned later that the seat belt — she wasn't wearing

a shoulder strap — had dissected her descending aorta, and she had bled almost her full volume of blood into her belly. There was nothing we could've done to help.

The poet Rainer Maria Rilke wrote, "So many live on and want nothing, and are raised to the rank of prince by the slippery ease of their light judgments."

That was Laurie and I in the beginning. We had donned the mantle of firefighters and thought — by the ease of our light judgments — that we understood.

For me, it wasn't until the call with the mom that the gravity of our calling resonated.

To be honest, after that call I wanted to quit. Rites of passage can be like that, too hard, so difficult that the other side, where you want to be, seems unimaginable — distant and impossible to reach. A rite of passage involves deconstructing who you once were; you are unmoored and adrift.

I spent a few months deconstructed as life went on around me, but there was this powerful counterweight: the community of the fire department. They pulled me back in and helped me understand that the point of a rite of passage is that you gain a deeper comprehension of your role, of your purpose.

Rilke continued, "But what you love to see are faces that do work and feel thirst. You love most of all those who need you as they need a crowbar or hoe."

To be needed. To do right work. To be useful in the face of hardship and tragedy; that is our purpose here. I awoke one morning a few months after this call and understood a bit more of what the work was and how powerful the pull was to be needed as a crowbar or hoe is needed.

If we are lucky, we will each experience a passage from

the light judgments of "childhood" to usefulness. We will seek a passage from comfort to purpose. We will cross the river from childhood to meaning. Often it takes tragedy, often it is painful, but it is the way. It is how we become who we are meant to be.

The trick of part 1 is obvious. There is no such thing as a firefighter universe. There is just the one universe we all share. Firefighters, I contend, just see it more clearly. It is illuminated for us every time we respond to a 911 call, whether it be comedic or tragic.

The goal, once we see it more clearly, is to live here calmly and passionately, with great purpose and usefulness, to accept the universe for what it is rather than what we wish it to be.

CHAPTER SEVEN

ON DYING

Life is uncertain. Death is certain.

— BUDDHA

I am not obsessed with death and dying. It is just something I know is on the horizon, waiting there for you, me, all of us. Of course — maybe like you — I am afraid. But we can learn to be scared and practical at the same time.

Once I was driving home in the middle of the night in the middle of nowhere in New Mexico. (Not the end of the world, but you can see it from there.) Out of the blue, I was struck by the knowledge I was going to die. It was visceral. I felt terror and a sense of loss. The terror of knowing that when you're dead, it is over for infinity. And loss for my family, knowing that I would miss them terribly, even though when you're dead you don't miss anything. There is no "you" anymore. Yet the feeling of loss was very real in that moment.

While all this was happening, I still had to drive the car: stay in my lane, drive exactly five miles an hour over the speed limit, and not hit anyone.

This is what I want to discuss. While we are alive, we can

panic, weep, and despair about our own death, but we still need to plan for our demise, if only to avoid chaos for those we love. We still have to drive the car.

Preparing for your eventual death — anticipating the dying process and the after-death arrangements — is an act of compassion. The death of a loved one is a tragedy — the most challenging event any of us will experience. Specifying important details (like finances) ahead of time will help avoid conflict and confusion and give loved ones more time and space to grieve.

Fear, denial, and discomfort often keep us from thinking about and planning for our own death. Fear of death, unless you're a Zen master, is natural: fear of being incapacitated, in pain, in a nursing home, dying in an ICU. We can't know what will happen to us. A glitch might take us in an instant, or disease might make our death prolonged and agonizing. But we will die, and we can anticipate various practical concerns about the dying process.

To be blunt, I encourage you to face any discomfort you feel about talking to your children, spouse, or friends about how you want to die and pushing through it. This conversation is hard, it's sad, there may be tears, but it's meaningful and helpful for everyone.

In our fire department, when we talk about death and dying among ourselves, the most common sentiment is that we don't want to be a burden to our families. We've seen the exhaustion, the tears, the caregivers at the end of their ropes. We don't want to put our families through that. Some take this to an extreme. One firefighter mentioned that when he knows it's his time, he wants to take a bottle of vodka and disappear into the snow, rather than have his family subjected to watching him waste away.

That was part of a dark, late-at-night-returning-from-another-call firefighter soliloquy, but the motivation was the same one we all need in order to discuss this: Our compassion for our loved ones can overcome fear, denial, and discomfort.

It can seem like a steep mountain to climb. Loved ones can feel their own resistance. Spouses often say, "I don't want to have this conversation." If that happens, persevere. It is an act of loving-kindness to make a plan.

Field Notes: On Dying

1. Begin planning for your death while you're still a healthy adult — say, in your forties. Buy insurance that covers end-of-life care; your loved ones will thank you later.

2. As you get older, heed Henry David Thoreau's words: "Simplify, simplify, simplify." It is a hard task for survivors to sort through someone's possessions, so make it easier for them. Prune and organize what you have, and get rid of junk. Make Goodwill your friend! Enjoy simplicity!

3. Legalize a will that clearly spells out how your "estate" and possessions will be distributed after your death (to avoid probate!). If you wish, specify who should do your eulogy. Trust me, little things matter.

4. Organize all your important papers, files, and passwords in one place. Accessing your vital information should be easy once you're gone, not a wild-goose chase.

5. Draft an end-of-life plan that spells out how you

want to be treated once you are dying. For example, would you rather be in a hospice center or at home with family? What can you afford? (See #1.) What can your family or a loved one manage? Be realistic: End-of-life care can be exhausting for a surviving spouse or caregiver. Will they need help? What is the most compassionate decision?

6. Specify if you want a funeral or a family gathering to commemorate you after death. Remember: You won't be there, so think about what is best for your loved ones.

7. Specify if you want to be buried or cremated. Anticipate costs and make sure your family knows your wishes.

8. Legally appoint someone to be your health-care decision maker when and if you are unable to decide what kind of care you need.

9. If you become critically sick, or fear becoming incapacitated, legalize a DNR (a do-not-resuscitate order) that clearly spells out which treatments under what conditions are appropriate and which are not. Remember, in a 911 situation, first responders are obligated to attempt resuscitation unless there is a legal DNR telling them not to. If appropriate, post the DNR on your fridge.

10. Have a conversation with your family and loved ones about all these issues. Ask for their thoughts and concerns and include them in your decisions.

part two

KEEP CALM
AND CARRY ON

Remain calm, serene, always
in command of yourself. You
will then find out how easy it
is to get along.

— PARAMAHANSA YOGANANDA

"Keep Calm and Carry On" was first used on a poster at the beginning of World War II in England. It was designed to call out the best of the British at a time when it was thought a German invasion was imminent. The attack never came, the poster was never used, and it was lost to history until a copy surfaced in an obscure Northern England bookstore. Since then, it has become iconic and often copied.

The message, as clichéd as it might seem, resonates with firefighters. We cannot be panicked or upset and do our jobs.

Firefighters, by training and experience, learn to be calm and carry on under often arduous circumstances.

As the phrase implies, this requires two abilities. The first is learning how to frame events, and the second is learning how to deal with stress in the moment.

To the extent that we can stay calm, solve problems, and not get upset every time our pagers go off, we have a much better shot at not getting burned out and overwhelmed by traumatic situations.

To be clear: "Being calm" doesn't mean refusing to feel. It doesn't mean forgoing joy or excitement or denying fear. Instead, it means taking life as it comes as serenely as possible.

Enjoy moments that are to be enjoyed, and don't overreact when things don't go right. Don't get hijacked by anger every time someone cuts you off on the interstate. This is a skill that improves our entire life.

It took Laurie and me a while to understand how to manage all that comes at you on the department. In the beginning, we were adrenaline junkies.

CHAPTER EIGHT

ADRENALINE JUNKIES

Life goes by fast. Enjoy it. Calm down. It's all funny.
Next. Everyone gets so upset about the wrong
things.

— JOAN RIVERS

One summer evening I was sitting at home with our three-month-old daughter on my lap when the pager went off.

REEEE! "Hondo, car crash with injuries. I-25 at mile marker 282."

I jumped up yelling into the bedroom where Laurie was napping, "Laurie, car crash! Gotta go!"

I popped our daughter onto the bed next to a sleepy Laurie and took off. I had just committed the mortal sin of waking a sleeping new mom from her first nap in days. I knew there would be retribution. But I was a firefighter!

We lived down a three-mile country dirt road and five miles from our station, so in my new firefighter brain, speed was essential, as were emergency lights and sirens, even though there was never anyone on our road.

Charged with adrenaline, I sprinted out the front door,

then abruptly shifted to a casual saunter. This was to distract my nemeses, our dogs, who had learned that me sprinting to the car was their cue to race me down the road. It was their favorite game, but it was distracting and dangerous. Even though my heart was racing, I played it cool as I attempted phase one: sneak attack and grab their collars so I could drag them inside. It rarely worked. They could smell the adrenaline. They let me get within inches and then sprinted away, their tongues hanging out the sides of their grinning mouths. Desperate, I escalated to phase two: herd them back to the house. Watching a human attempt herding is highly entertaining to German shepherds.

Defeated by their canine craftiness, my anxiety increasing, I finally said, "Shit!" and jumped into the car. I was now fully committed to phase three: driving so fast that they would give up before I reached the first switchback on our road.

It's incredible how fast German shepherds are. They ran alongside me, no doubt thinking, *This is the best you can do?*

I finally put some distance between us, and they gave up and sat on the road, panting. Of course, I was driving too fast, spun out, and glanced off a piñon tree. In my defense, that tree was way too close to the road. "Shit," I swore again, backing up the Subaru and charging forward. Now I would have to explain to Laurie the latest dent in the car. At least twice before as Laurie and I responded to calls together, and I tried mightily to negotiate the switchbacks, she would yell, "Trees!" This time she wasn't with me, I missed the corner, and *whack!*

My heart was pumping. A few minutes later, as I finally hit the asphalt, the dispatcher came on the radio, "Hondo, cancel the call, cancel. It's just an abandoned car."

I pulled over, put my head on the steering wheel, closed

my eyes, and swore that I was going to get a chain saw and cut down that tree.

I was an adrenaline junkie. I was addicted to the excitement and thrill that rushed through me whenever we got a call.

Adrenaline is a powerful drug. We called it Saint Adrenaline for the effect it has. When you've been pulled from a warm bed in the middle of a winter's night, it will give you the strength to do things you normally couldn't imagine doing, and it gives you armor that protects against the worst things you will see.

Like all addictive drugs, it comes with a cost. First, you don't make the best decisions when adrenalized: You race dogs and run into trees for no real reason. Whether I sped down our dirt road at fifty miles an hour with lights and siren on, or just calmly drove the speed limit (a lot less than fifty), I'd end up getting to the scene within a few minutes, but one way I wouldn't be banging into trees. Next, it's exhausting. The "comedown" from adrenaline is steep and can leave you feeling numb.

Truth be told, there are more than a few adrenaline junkies in the first-responder world. Once, two of us were treating a chest-pain patient. The call had gone out as a cardiac arrest, but when we arrived, the patient was alert and talking. As we were administering oxygen and getting ready to transport, a paramedic bound through the door, roaring, "My patient!" He was fully committed to running a cardiac arrest code without noticing that the patient was, well, alive.

Finally, along with adrenaline comes irrationality and irritation. Adrenaline does not bring out our best selves. Our responses in a crisis can become inappropriate and unhelpful. We snap at each other. I've even seen fights break out.

This applies to any crisis in everyday life. We live in highly adrenalized and stressful times, no matter what your personal circumstances or political persuasion. Politically, socially, personally, and professionally — pick one — our current world seems to be continually erupting in crisis.

Marshall McLuhan, presciently, wrote decades ago that "the medium is the message." It isn't just the content that we read that affects us. The media itself, the way we receive information, has the power to impact us. And look at us now! We can hold in one hand a window to everything that is happening in the world. News, mostly unfortunate, streams at us continuously. Smartphones are like a firefighter's pager ringing out every minute. Do we respond by charging down the road in a fury, or do we become benumbed by it all and barely able to move?

If the goal is to "keep calm and carry on," neither response helps. However, here's the good news: It is good to be an old firefighter. After a few years, the adrenaline response fades and one learns how to deal with the pager going off, with the sounds of sirens and pleas for help. One learns how not to burn out or go crazy even when everyone around you is at their wit's end.

Anyone can learn this ability. The first step is understanding the role problems and crises play in our lives, why we continually have them, and what we do about them. To begin, let's visit a certain Zen master.

CHAPTER NINE

THE EIGHTY-SEVENTH PROBLEM

What you're supposed to do when you don't like a thing is change it. If you can't change it, change the way you think about it. Don't complain.

— MAYA ANGELOU

There is a Zen story about a wealthy man searching for answers to a pressing problem. He's told that a certain Zen master might have the answer. He sells all his possessions to finance the trip and sets out on an immediate search. It takes him years. He searches all the continents. Finally, with patience gone and wealth disappearing, he climbs one more mountain and finds the master in a small cabin.

Joyously, he knocks on the door.

"Enter," an old voice creaks.

The man enters and says, "Master, I've been looking for you for so long!"

The old man answers, "I know. And I know why you're here."

Taken aback, the man asks, "How could you know why I'm here?"

Chuckling, the master replies, "You're here because you have a problem."

The man, now a bit impatient — after all, he has spent his fortune and many years trying to find this master — sternly asks, "How do you know I have a problem?"

The master shrugs. "Because we all have problems. To be precise, we all have exactly eighty-six problems. Each time we solve one, the universe gives us another one so that we always have eighty-six problems. Exactly, precisely, eighty-six."

The man becomes frustrated and anxious. Unending problems? He had started his search with just one problem, and now he finds out that he has eighty-six?

His shoulders sag.

"Oh, yes," the master continues, "there is also an eighty-seventh problem."

The man rubs his head, closes his eyes, and grimaces.

"And what is that?" he asks.

The master cackles. "The eighty-seventh problem is believing you shouldn't have problems."

The man, now thoroughly discouraged, gets up to leave.

"My son," the master says, seeing the frustration on the man's face, "let me give you this most important advice. Our task is not to complain and whine that we have problems. Our task is to continually solve the problems we face. Eat, laugh, sleep. Then get up the next day and solve more problems. And on and on until you're done having problems."

The master again cackles. "'Done having problems' is called death."

The fire department pager is an interesting device. It's a "problem announcer." The loud and screeching tone lets us know at any time of day or night that there is a problem. In the beginning — like our first call — it startled us when it toned out. After a few years, however, it became background noise. It's no longer surprising, day or night, that there is a page, that someone has a problem, that someone is in trouble.

The realization dawns that as long as there are humans, there will be problems: Dog knocks over space heater, house burns down. Desiccated body in the mountains. Dead guy in a car with pants down around his knees, woman staggering down the road wearing nothing but a bolo tie. The list is endless because there are always eighty-six problems.

A problem is the difference between what you have and what you want.

And problems are unpredictable both in terms of when and what.

Once, after a few years in the department, I sat down and tried to come up with a way to predict when calls would happen. For example, on the Fourth of July, I anticipated brush fires because of fireworks. When it snowed during rush hour, we were sure to have car crashes. When the bars close at 1 AM, we could bet on drunk drivers causing more crashes. My algorithm predicted that Sunday mornings would be quiet and Saturday nights busy. I predicted that most house fires would happen during the fall when people were using their fireplaces for the first time in the season. I color-coded the entire plan, intending to hang it up in our kitchen.

Proud of my work, I showed it to Laurie. She looked at me and said, "Let's just not show that to anyone. It will be our secret."

She was right. There is no predictability. Houses burn down all year around. A drunk mom crashes her car after dropping her kids off at school. Brush fires light up in April, and the Fourth of July is quiet. One of the worst crashes we had was on a lazy Sunday morning.

Problems are ubiquitous and often unpredictable — they arrive out of the blue. Accepting that fact — being grounded in the idea that we will always have eighty-six problems and our task is to continually solve them — is crucial for our mental health.

This line of thought raises objections. First, we crave problem-free lives. We think that not having problems is synonymous with happiness, and that having problems is the opposite of happiness. Neither is true. Satisfaction often comes from dealing with problems, solving them, and moving on to the next one. Are there problems we cannot solve? Yes, and we will deal with those subsequently.

Then, as the Zen master instructed, wishing for no problems, believing we shouldn't have problems, is the eighty-seventh problem. This arises from the belief that somehow, someway, we don't deserve the challenges and crises we face. We think it is not fair, not reasonable.

And it isn't! On the department, we see individuals who've been beaten up by life, who have a litany of problems that would bring most of us to our knees.

But the universe is neither fair nor reasonable. It makes

no sense how it works. One person is burdened by calamity and another misses a train and complains about being late for work.

Another important joke: A man wakes up in the morning, gets out of bed, and trips on a toy, spraining his ankle. Hopping on one foot, he bangs into the doorframe and drops to his knees. The phone rings. It's his boss, telling him he's been laid off. He crawls into the kitchen and lifts himself. On the table he finds a note from his wife that reads, "I'm leaving you and taking the kids!" He drops back to his knees and pleads, "God, why are you doing this to me?"

A dry and sardonic voice answers, "Because I had a bad day."

Capricious, unfair, and not reasonable. Trying to find logic behind who has what problem is often a fool's errand.

We can be shocked by the magnitude of a problem, but not by the fact that problems happen, not by the fact that the pager goes off in the middle of the night, in the middle of work, in the middle of dinner, when we are doing other things. Stuff happens whether we like it or not.

Given the ubiquity of problems, it makes no sense to resist them. To complain that they shouldn't happen. It's complaining about the weather. Fun to do, the ultimate ice-breaker, but useless. And I don't mean never complain about the rain. Stop complaining when it's a form of resistance. As the Zen master advised, focus your time and energy on solving the problems you face, not wishing them away.

I have often wondered if there was more to the story of the man and the eighty-six problems. Was he enlightened after his meeting with the Zen master, or did he become bitter? I choose to believe that a light turned on for him. I imagine he solved his eighty-seventh problem and lessened his burden to just the other eighty-six. He returned to the path of solving his problems rather than wondering why he had them.

That is our challenge, too: to let go of the frustration that we have problems, to realize — as we do on the fire department — that as long as there are people, there will be 911 calls. Just answer the pager and get on with solving the next problem as serenely as possible.

Of course, we haven't discussed the magnitude of problems. There is a difference between getting a speeding ticket and getting a cancer diagnosis. There is a difference between the small and the life-bending.

CHAPTER TEN

EMERGENCIES, PROBLEMS, AND INCONVENIENCES

To be mature means to face, and not evade, every
fresh crisis that comes.

— FRITZ KÜNKEL

REEEE! "Hondo respond to 29 Apache Ridge Road.
Forty-three-year-old female, difficulty breathing."

We rattled up the rutted dirt road in our ambulance,
hoping that we'd get there in time to do some good.

As we pulled in the driveway, we were greeted by a woman
standing outside the house. The wind was blowing; there was
dust in the air. It was midafternoon in June in Santa Fe.

Three of us walked up to the woman, tall and lanky, wearing a work shirt, jeans, and worn cowboy boots. We figured
that she wasn't the patient because she seemed fine.

Then she spoke.

"I'm house-sitting here. The cleaning woman used an in-
dustrial cleaner when she cleaned the oven. I have chemical
sensitivities, and I can't go back to the kitchen. Can you guys
clean the oven for me? And just use water and soap?"

Dan, our chief, rolled his eyes. But another firefighter, Barbara, looked from us to the woman and said, "Sure."

Barbara recruited me, and we walked into the kitchen and spent the next fifteen minutes cleaning the oven. Just to be safe and not get paged back to the same house, we also did the stove top.

Finished, we walked out, and the woman asked for us to wait while she went to check our work. She returned a minute later, thanked us, and went back in the house.

Dan rolled his eyes again; we got back in the ambulance, reported to dispatch "mission accomplished," and went back to the station.

This kind of call is not uncommon. In fact, the majority of our calls — 90 percent — are similar in that they are not really emergencies, at least not to us.

When your business is emergencies, you develop a scale for what constitutes an emergency.

One call sums this up. It went out as "baby not breathing." That definitely qualifies as an emergency, and we responded as quickly as we could. When we arrived, Laurie and Dan ran toward the house, and I followed with our gear. The dad met us at the door and told us their baby had started to breathe again and was actually crying. In fact, in our world, a crying baby is most often a healthy baby — it is a beautiful sound. We immediately calmed down. We checked the baby out, all seemed fine, and they decided to drive their child to their pediatrician just to be safe. As we packed up to leave, the dad said, "It's nice to know that our emergency is just your regular day."

A baby not breathing is and will always be a "ten" on my scale of emergencies, but I took his point. Everyone has their own scale. First responders, because of what they see, have their own, almost unique perspective, which I'd summarize like this:

There are emergencies, there are problems, and there are inconveniences. To us, the "baby not breathing" call shifted immediately from an emergency to a minor problem, maybe even an inconvenience, but to the father, it remained an emergency. And this is what we often see: People get their scale and their response mixed up. They treat problems and inconveniences like emergencies and then panic, when they could focus their energy on solving the problem or just taking the inconveniences in stride.

Down the Rabbit Hole

First responders don't adopt this perspective consciously or all at once; it isn't a choice you necessarily make. It arises through the ongoing experience of dealing with every sort of problem imaginable, up and down the scale. Knowing how bad things can be, we start wondering why people get so upset all the time. Sometimes it feels like we must be missing something. Sometimes it feels, as firefighters, that we are so far down the rabbit hole that we are out of touch with typical day-to-day living. We wonder: If people could see what we see day in and day out, would they revise their scale and remain calmer in their regular lives? If they could spend a night running with us to a few DWI crashes, would it help them realize that most problems are not tragedies and not worth getting truly upset over? It certainly worked that way for me.

Today, I can say flat out: To me, an emergency is not a child coming home with a bad report card, being overlooked for a promotion, or having the flu. These are problems to be solved, surely. Being stuck in traffic, missing a flight? These are simply inconveniences — bumps in the road.

I'm not laid back by nature, but the litany of real emergencies and tragedies I've been exposed to has changed my perspective: cardiac arrests, families losing their homes to fires, car crashes with multiple fatalities. As a result, it is hard to get upset over a high utility bill, a broken water heater, a child not making the soccer team. I don't like problems and inconveniences, but they no longer raise my temperature.

This, of course, is my perspective. Everyone has their own perspective and scale based on their own experience. But here is something else that my time as a firefighter has taught me: Real emergencies are rare. Most of the calls we go on are problems or inconveniences. No one is badly hurt or sick; no house is being stricken by the dragon, fire.

I believe the same ratio applies universally, and we can use it to help guide our responses in our daily lives. Yes, by profession, firefighters make themselves ready to respond to emergencies, but they learn that most of the time people call for a problem or an inconvenience, not a crisis, and so we learn to adjust our response immediately to match the situation.

Our First Response: Self-Talk

Why is this distinction important? The answer is our self-talk. When something happens, and our internal pager tones out, we immediately evaluate and respond based on what we tell ourselves.

For example, if my firefighter pager announces a cardiac arrest, my first thought is "This is an emergency!" and I respond accordingly: I'm going to drive fast to arrive as quick as possible and go to work to save a life.

If a call arrives as a "sick call" — which means someone is using the ambulance just to be transported to the hospital in a nonemergency — my self-talk is quite different: "Not urgent. I can drive at a reasonable speed and still get the work done."

The problem is, if we are not managing our self-talk, we can go into "emergency" mode for events that are not life and death. This can cause us to overreact by treating a relatively insignificant problem like a full-blown crisis, which can make things worse.

For instance, we were once paged to a trash fire at a home. Not a big deal. But one of our new members, who had just gotten lights and sirens on his car, lost control of his response. He treated it like an emergency, rushed to the scene, missed the turn onto the road, and crashed into, you guessed it, a tree.

The key is realizing that our internal pager will go off for any reason — emergency, problem, or inconvenience — and only rarely will it be a true emergency. We have to evaluate before responding. If we tell ourselves, "This is an emergency," we will become adrenalized and upset. If, however, we take the time to evaluate the issue on our scale and recognize when something is just a "problem" or only an "inconvenience," then we not only tend to stay calmer, but our response remains appropriate and effective.

I often do this when my pager goes off to avoid getting ramped up for no reason. I ask myself, "Is this an emergency, a problem to be solved, or an inconvenience?" You can do the same thing whenever anything happens in everyday life:

- Is a bad report card an emergency, problem, or inconvenience?
- Is a missed flight an emergency, problem, or inconvenience?
- Is a lost work opportunity an emergency, problem, or inconvenience?
- Is being laid off an emergency, problem, or inconvenience?
- Is being dumped an emergency, problem, or inconvenience?

In theory, which you choose depends on your circumstances. A missed flight or being fired could qualify as emergencies in rare situations, but most often they are only problems or just inconveniences. If lives aren't at stake, if health and welfare aren't in dire jeopardy, most situations can be overcome: We can improve our grades, get another flight, find another job, find another partner. These are just some of the eighty-six problems that are ours to solve. When we treat them that way, solutions come easier and our lives are more peaceful.

In fact, I find myself thinking, *This is inconvenient* a lot. I highly recommend it. When something happens, look around. If everyone is basically okay, say to yourself, "This is just an inconvenience." When you feel yourself getting ramped up because traffic isn't moving, whisper to yourself, "This is not an emergency; it is just an inconvenience." When the copy machine stops working at 5 PM on a Friday, just say, "More inconvenience." When you fix it by 6 PM, and your boss calls you in to talk, think, "Only inconvenience."

Say it out loud; think it often. You'll be surprised at the effect this one word can have.

Field Notes: On Inconveniences

1. Take one day and list all the things that happen that upset you. From stuff at home to work issues to your commute. Just make a list for that day.
2. That night go through your list and label each one. Was it an emergency, a problem to be solved, or an inconvenience? Use the test: Was anyone seriously injured or sick? Was a long-term plan put in jeopardy? Was your emotional or physical security threatened (or that of a loved one)?
3. Consider each label and ask yourself if you responded appropriately each time. Did you get ramped up and overreact, treating an inconvenience like a problem, or a problem like an emergency?
4. Periodically, keep practicing this exercise. Over time, it will increase your self-awareness and help you stay calm and respond more appropriately to the things that go wrong — the eighty-six problems — every day.

CHAPTER ELEVEN

NOT MY EMERGENCY

If you want to go fast, go slow.

— BRUCE WOLLENS, Hondo VFD

On any emergency scene, I want to be calm. I want to be present, and I want to be creative. I want to be composed so that I — we — can see the problem and all possible solutions. I sometimes need out-of-the-box ideas, like how to disentangle a car from a bridge abutment or how to get a large man with intense back pain out of his bathroom and down three flights of stairs.

Being a firefighter has taught me that being efficient, curious, and creative are often as important as following the book.

To that end, firefighters have all sorts of tools — mental ones — to help find the "sweet spot" when we respond to an emergency scene.

I think you will find these tools useful in all sorts of situations when the goal is to stay calm and creative when everyone around you is losing their heads.

Pause, Breathe, and Take Your Pulse

REEEE! "Hondo, structure fire, flames showing. Possible explosion."

When the pager goes off, the first thing I do is start breathing. It sounds simple, but deep, purposeful breathing is the pathway to calm.

Whether you are a Zen practitioner, a runner, a weight lifter, or a firefighter, controlling your breath is how you move from anxiety to performance, from tense to relaxed.

The overriding goal is to slow your breathing down and focus on four to six deep, slow breaths. I like to use "square breathing," which is simple to remember:

1. Two seconds: inhale
2. Two seconds: hold your breath
3. Two seconds: exhale
4. Two seconds: hold
5. Repeat for four to six breaths

This is a skill we can practice regularly. Get up in the morning, square breathing. Stuck in traffic, breathe. Before you walk into your home after work (the whirling hour)… breathe. Once it becomes a habit, you'll notice that after the first breath you'll start to relax, your shoulders will drop, and you'll be able to think more clearly.

This is just a way to follow the old fire-service cliché: Take your own pulse before you take the pulse of a patient. Before acting, take a few seconds to calm down and slow down.

These are great strategies in a crisis. Pause for a moment, take four to six deep breaths, take your own pulse, and you'll be able to think more clearly and be more productive.

Repeat Mantras

Banging down a dirt road to a car crash, I can feel myself getting ramped up. Adrenaline flowing, my foot getting heavier on the gas pedal. Right about then, I repeat to myself my favorite mantras. They slow me down and help me think.

I believe in mantras — short memorized statements that help me stay calm and focused.

The first is simple: *This is not my emergency.*

When firefighters respond to a call, no matter how serious, we drum into our brains that — while this might be an emergency for the person, the patient, the owner of a house on fire — it isn't our illness, injury, or home burning. We can be empathetic, but we don't want to absorb and reflect back someone else's panic. *It's not our emergency.* It's our job, we train for it, and most likely we've seen it or something like it before.

Similarly, when you are in a crisis situation, it's essential to ask the question, "Whose emergency is this?"

The patients or the victims — the ones who are directly affected — this is their emergency. But it's not for everyone else around them: family, friends, first responders, and even bystanders. It is crucial to understand and define your role in a crisis. Is this your emergency or someone else's? Are you the victim who needs help or is your role to solve the problem or provide support? I think of crises as the rock thrown in the pond, and the waves ripple outward in concentric circles. The individual or individuals who are the actual victims or patients are in the center of the circle, that inner circle again. Everyone else is part of an outer circle with a different role; it is not their emergency. They are there to help, not to panic.

If it is not your emergency, pause, breathe, calm down, take your pulse first, and help solve the problem.

The second mantra is just as simple: *Go slow to go fast*.

When we rush, we make mistakes, and mistakes cost time. When I'm on a scene, especially a complex one, I repeat this endlessly. If I slow down, check that I have the right medication, make sure that I've grabbed the right end of a hose line (seriously), then I actually save time. Nothing is more frustrating than having to repeat steps because I've zoomed and forgotten something.

In a crisis, go slow when you can. Think about what you're doing. Don't scream out of the house to the hospital, forgetting your insurance card or to lock the house. It will save time: *Go slow to go fast*.

My third mantra is: *Sick or not sick?*

I use this mantra once I've arrived on the scene, when I need to step back and decide what's most urgent. When we receive a 911 call, we've learned not to trust the information we get. It's not the dispatcher's fault, nor is it the caller's. Instead, in an emergency, information often gets left out, garbled, ignored, or exaggerated — and what we've been told to expect isn't always what we find at the scene. We roll into a call that went out as a cardiac arrest and are greeted by a talking and alert patient complaining of acid reflux.

We've learned to be suspicious of any call and to walk in with our eyes open.

Once we've determined that a scene is safe, we consider each person involved and ask, "Sick or not sick?"

"Sick" means an emergency; whether a person is suffering from trauma or an illness, we are going to transport them immediately. "Not sick" means someone has a problem, even an inconvenience, and we are going to remain on the scene, take our time, calm everyone down, and get to the bottom of what is going on. For example, a "sick" patient might have chest pains, where a "not sick" patient might be an adult with a fever.

Use these mantras when something happens in your life: Is it your emergency or not? If not, calm down, and go slow to go fast. Then ask, Sick or not sick? Does something need immediate attention or can it wait?

Turn On the Switch

All these tools — the discipline of breathing, taking your own pulse, and the mantras — are part of the firefighter mindset. When the pager rings out, the switch turns on, and a normal dad becomes a firefighter.

But as I've gotten older, with grown-up kids, with elderly parents, and with the fraught politics we've inherited, that switch gets turned on in civilian life more and more. It's useful: breathing, calming down, using those mantras. They work not only at a fire but when crisis hits our family or when broadcast news (or Twitter) erupts with inflammatory events and opinions.

Most people never have to attack a house fire at 2 AM, but we all have plenty of "fires" in our lives. That is as near a guarantee as the universe makes.

At a fire, firefighters automatically grab the tools off the engine that they know they will probably need: an ax, a pry bar, an SCBA (self-contained breathing apparatus). Yet in any difficult, stressful situation, we can always grab these mental tools: deep breathing, a calming mantra. Even repeating to yourself "I will not get upset" will do.

No one ever perfects this, but we can get better. The goal isn't to become a Zen master, but to approach life's emergencies with the intention to remain calm and act creatively.

Once we responded to a multiple-vehicle crash, with one car on top of another and another rolled over. Initially, as it often is in the beginning, everything was chaos. Then a paramedic stepped out of the ambulance, looked around, actually yawned, and sized up the scene. I remember wanting to be that calm, that composed. So I copied him. I stretched, put my hands in my pockets, and looked around. Then we went to work. I noted how just that one calm paramedic took all the anxiety out of the scene, and we got the job done effectively and with only a little craziness. He became my mental model for how to act.

Calm. Serene. Effective. Creative.

CHAPTER TWELVE

THE ZEN OF FIREFIGHTING

I believe that only one person in a thousand knows the trick of really living in the present. Most of us spend fifty-nine minutes an hour living in the past, with regret for lost joys or shame for things badly done (both utterly useless and weakening) or in a future which we either long for or dread.

Yet the past is gone beyond prayer, and every minute you spend in a vain effort to anticipate the future is a moment lost. There is only one world, the world pressing against you at this minute. There is only one minute in which you are alive, this minute, here and now. The only way to live is by accepting each minute as an unrepeatable miracle. Which is exactly what it is — a miracle and unrepeatable.

— MARGARET STORM JAMESON

There is an ineffable quality to the sense of being present. For firefighters, it can happen on the most intense scenes; world and time collapse around a house fire. There are all the familiar smells of smoke and fire. There are the sounds of radios crackling. There are the actions of pulling lines off engines, taking tools, and saws being started. Assignments are given: Take a window out, knock down the fire. Be the entry team, hose line, tools at the ready, the adrenaline of waiting to meet the dragon. There is the physical labor of it all.

In these moments there is only the present. There is no yesterday or tomorrow. There is just now, in this battle.

This becomes both paradox and promise. On the one hand, structure fires are singular, infrequent events. On the other hand, being that present in the moment is a powerful experience, one that becomes a craving.

Here is the promise: The experience of being present in the moment is open to us anytime…if we are open to it.

However, some moments are more conducive to being present than others. In my nonfirefighter world, I have three regular times when I can focus on the "now." The first is being in the wilderness. The second is with my family in the evenings. Finally, there is the time spent with my granddaughter.

These times lend themselves to being present and mindful.

When and where are the times in your daily life that you can be present — not ruminating about the past (which you can do nothing about) or worrying about the future (ditto)?

Even mundane tasks can be turned into mindful times. For example, one of the regular tasks we do on any fire department is wash trucks. It is a point of pride to have clean vehicles. In doing so, I have a choice every Saturday morning. I can think that this is an annoying and ridiculous task — the trucks will just become dirty over a week of calls. I can work while being caught up in a million different worries, not even aware of what I am doing.

Or I can choose to be mindful; I can realize that all over the country, firefighters are washing trucks, and I am part of this great community. I can allow myself to become absorbed in the task, the sound of water, the camaraderie of the firehouse, the feel of a soapy sponge, the look of a truck as it reappears clean and shining. The choice is mine. One path can lead to boredom and even despair (such as the thought of doing this every Saturday for decades). One decision leads to fulfillment. Life is full of mundane and sometimes absurd tasks when we can practice being in the moment, being present.

The ultimate goal, of course, is to live our lives in the "now." To be present through joy, pain, and sorrow, to be right there.

I have learned this lesson dozens of times. After demanding late-night calls, I would sneak into my daughters' room, sit on the floor, and just listen to them breathe. Again, I felt the ineffable sense of time and space collapsing and me just being there. I would often have no sense of how long I stayed. But it would bring me peace and the precious sense that for that moment everything was all right.

Field Notes: Seize the Moment

Here are a couple of suggestions for helping to capture and stay in the moment:

1. Turn off the alerts and mute your smartphone. Ignore your social media.

2. Choose to immerse yourself in the details of the moment. On walks, I make a point of listening to the sounds and seeing the details of the landscape around me. With my family, I focus on how much I love them, on the sound of their voices, on how their day went, and especially on the sound of their laughter.

3. As worries or planning come into your mind (which they will), just let them go. Sometimes if an idea pops into my brain, I'll make a list, so I don't worry that I'll forget it. Then I let it go.

4. Breathing (again!) becomes my cue to stay in the moment. When I find myself drifting off into worries and concerns, I focus on my breathing (see "square breathing," page 88) to bring me back.

CHAPTER THIRTEEN

STAYING CALM: A PRIMER

Between stimulus and response there is a space.
In that space is our power to choose our response.
In our response lies our growth and our freedom.

— ROLLO MAY

The singular and most important idea that will help us stay calm in an emergency — or at any other time — is that we have a choice.

It often doesn't feel like we have a choice. Something happens, we get rear-ended on the highway, and we are quick to anger. We think the guy that hit us made us angry! That happens so fast in our minds that we link the event (being hit) to the consequence (our anger).

In other words, we think being hit caused our anger.

That is a troubling statement, for it implies that we have no choice in the matter. Something happens, and I respond in one way; something happens again, and I must respond again and again in the same way.

This assumption of cause and effect is built into our language:

- My kids make me mad.
- My girlfriend (or boyfriend) drives me crazy.
- The traffic makes me impatient.

When we use and believe this language, we set ourselves up to be ping-pong balls in life, reacting to one event after another. We become like Pavlov's dogs, salivating every time the bell rings and saying to ourselves, "It's that darn bell!"

Intuitively, we know that is not true. Intuitively, we know that we can influence our thinking and choose how to act. For example, if another motorist hits our car, our immediate reaction might be fear and shock. Something unexpected and dangerous has happened. If we are physically unhurt, what happens next? Do we become angry, blaming the other driver for doing something wrong? Do we jump out to see if the other driver is okay, since they might be hurt? Do we restore our own sense of calm and simply be grateful it wasn't more serious? We have a choice.

What is behind the choices we make? A quick illustration from the firefighter world:

Three firefighters respond to a cardiac arrest and perform CPR. Although they work the code by the book, the patient doesn't recover. Our first firefighter, an experienced paramedic, comforts the family by saying (and believing), "We did everything we could."

The second firefighter, a brand-new EMT, is upset at losing their first cardiac arrest patient. The person blames themselves and their training, thinking, *This is not the way it worked in class!* The third firefighter, the veteran chief, walks away depressed and discouraged, thinking, *I can't attend one more death, CPR never works…*

The cardiac arrest is the same; the CPR techniques and results are the same. So what caused the three different reactions? The diverse beliefs and thinking of each person.

To be nerdy for a moment, here is an "ABC" diagram of what happened:

$$\underline{A}\text{ctivating Event} \longrightarrow \underline{B}\text{eliefs} \longrightarrow \underline{C}\text{onsequences} = \text{in Emotions \& Actions}$$

The activating event is A; this is anything that happens that gets our attention. This is filtered by our beliefs (or B), which include our history, experiences, and worldview. Finally, the consequence (or C) is how we respond as a result: what we choose to feel and do.

Obviously, we are not in control of "A," the activating events. Stuff happens. The pager goes off in the middle of the night. Yet we can control our beliefs and attitude, our worldview. We can also recognize difficult emotions and choose how to manage them. Fear doesn't have to become anger and blame. Failure doesn't have to lead to self-doubt and discouragement. We can think: *The driver behind me just made a mistake. I've done it before myself. This is inconvenient, but it is not a tragedy.* Or: *CPR works 10 percent of the time in the field. It's not perfect, but it's the best we have.*

Our beliefs influence how we understand and respond to events. So if our responses are unhelpful, if we lose our cool, if difficulties invariably cause eruptions of anger, then we can adjust our thinking and beliefs and change how we respond in order to be more effective, helpful, and happier.

Stop, Challenge, and Choose

First, we have to acknowledge that our minds are not fact-finding, truth-telling computers. Instead, they are full of beliefs, assumptions, prejudices, stories, and ways to successfully navigate our worlds. In a phrase, we are all graduates from the University of Making Stuff Up. We get a couple of data points, and we generalize: *Hah! This is the way things are!*

Many of those beliefs, no matter how "off" they might be, go unchallenged throughout our lives.

To respond more effectively, then, our goal should be to continually examine our beliefs, test them against reality, and make sure they are accurate. In other words, to quit making stuff up!

That is the theory, and here is a tool for doing so that is called "Stop, Challenge, and Choose."

Stop: Whenever an "activating event" causes you to feel upset, stressed, or any negative emotion, stop. Either physically stop or get off the roller coaster of thoughts and feelings in your mind. Next, breathe and calm down. Try the "square breathing" exercise (page 88).

Challenge: Ask yourself, *What am I making up? What belief is causing me to be upset or stressed?* This can be hard work, but it is vital to understand what belief is causing your stress and upset.

Dr. Maxie Maultsby, the late American psychiatrist, suggested the following criteria for examining our beliefs (or what we might be making up):

1. Is my belief aligned with the facts?
2. Is it in my best short- and long-term interests?
3. Does it avoid unnecessary conflict with others?
4. Will my response help me feel the way I want to feel?

Choose: Choose a belief that is based on facts, that is in your best interests, that avoids unnecessary conflict, and that makes you feel the way you want to feel.

Once you've practiced Stop, Challenge, and Choose a few times, it becomes an automatic way to think, and it can take two minutes to apply.

As a firefighter, I use this during almost every call I go on. When I'm surrounded by upset people, and I can feel the tug of adrenaline, I stop, control my breathing, and challenge the thought, *Everyone is panicking; therefore, I should panic, too!* To calm myself, I often choose a mantra — like "This is not my emergency" or "Go slow to go fast."

When I consciously use this skill, I can show up the way I want to show up. This is the outcome we're looking for: to match our actions with what's needed in each moment or with the person we want to be.

part three

WHEN DRAGONS COME

Wisdom comes through suffering.

— AESCHYLUS, *Agamemnon*

In the epic eighth-century tale, the hero Beowulf battles and defeats the beast Grendel and later the mother of Grendel. Yet fifty years later, Beowulf meets his match and is defeated and killed by a poisonous dragon come from the grave.

Part 3 is about dragons, the 1 percent of events, the true catastrophes that are out there, waiting for us to either overcome them, defeat them, or be defeated. This part is about learning how to survive when dragons appear out of the earth to challenge us.

That's the question, isn't it? How do we go from lives of comfort and sometimes privilege, turn a corner, and then face the dragon? The dragon's role is to destroy you. Call it cancer, call it mental illness, call it a death, call it a fire that burns all your possessions. It is the same beast: It is personal, there for you only. And only you can deal with it.

That is where we are now. I must warn you that dragons are indefatigable. Sometimes you can defeat them; other times you accommodate them, learn to live with them. Other times they lay ruin and move on. Yet you can't eliminate them.

However, the thing we can't forget about dragons is that in their sack they carry not only suffering but growth.

This is not a bargain we want — having wisdom given to us in exchange for happiness or comfort — but when we confront dragons, that is the pact, the way it is. Every time you battle with a dragon — win, lose, or draw — you grow, you learn, you become stronger, even when you are temporarily brought to your knees.

In this part, I share what firefighters learn about being in the arena with dragons. From being prepared, to understanding suffering, to standing your ground, to getting under the smoke: I'll help you build emotional armor for the dragons you will face.

CHAPTER FOURTEEN

SOMETHING IS COMING TOWARD US

A society must assume that it is stable, but the artist must know, and he must let us know, that there is nothing stable under heaven.

— JAMES BALDWIN, "The Creative Process"

It was a bright Saturday morning in July, around our tenth year in the department. Dan and I were driving an engine back from a gas station. I mused that it had been so slow, hardly any calls for over two weeks. I seem to remember complaining that all we did was train, every Tuesday and Saturday, and yet we never seemed to use our skills. Dan thought a minute and remarked, "Look, there is something out there coming toward us that is going to fuck us up. It's just math. Our turn will come up. And you never know when it will happen or what it will be."

How, I thought, do you prepare for something, much less train for something, when you don't know what, when, or where?

Since this is a question that all of us face, I'm going to propose a couple of ways to think about it. The first starts with a story by Mark Twain, and it goes to the heart of how firefighters think.

In his book *Life on the Mississippi*, Twain wrote that growing up he thought of the river as this beautiful and poetic waterway. Yet as he trained to be a riverboat captain, he realized the same river was dangerous, full of snags and sandbars that could quickly sink a riverboat. The river was full of challenges and obstacles to be navigated in order to have a successful voyage. He had to know and read the river in an entirely different way: how snags roil in the current, how a bend that was navigable a month ago appeared sharper and foreboding in the gloaming.

The river doesn't change, but our perception of it does.

With the experience of a riverboat captain, he saw the river — the same river — with a different pair of glasses; both beautiful and perilous.

This is how I look at the geography of the mountains in the high desert. When Laurie and I moved here, I was taken by living in the forest three miles down a dead-end road. I marveled at the sense of isolation and the beautiful views. But now, after years on the department, what I see is how wildfires can consume these same picturesque homes and neighborhoods. A ravine is basically a chimney and will direct fire right to the home above it. The communities on those mountain roads have limited escape routes because they are all dead ends; there is only one way out.

In our first years, we would have been shocked and unprepared for a wildfire. Older and more experienced now, we think of wildfires as inevitable because fire is a constant presence in the West.

When you see the river and the mountains this way, of course, you're going to be more alert and more prepared.

Be it a sandbar or a wildfire, "something is out there coming toward us…"

Once you understand the geography of living, that "there is nothing stable under heaven," it becomes much easier to accept the premise that we need to be emotionally prepared.

What does that mean?

Here is a metaphor: Most athletes in most sports are taught the athletic stance — on the balls of your feet, knees slightly bent, arms out for balance, seeing the entire court or field. With this stance, an athlete is ready to move quickly in any direction, and it is hard to knock them off balance.

The geography of living requires us to have an emotional athletic stance, to know deep in our souls that nothing is permanent, and security is a myth. We have to be nimble, ready to move in any direction, ready to absorb any body blow without getting knocked senseless.

My Catholic mom would often express this idea when something good happened, as "waiting for the other shoe to drop." It was her way of keeping us on our toes and telling us not to assume that good luck would always follow us.

On the other hand, my father believed that everything works out, that luck is on our side.

Somewhere in between these polar opposite positions is the emotional athletic stance; alert for the whiff of smoke in the air, optimistic but ready for any problem that comes our way.

Nimble Means Adaptable

One advantage of the athletic stance is that the athlete is ready to move in any direction, depending on the opponent or the play. Ready to go forward, back, or sideways, to attack or defend. The same thing is key for emotional agility. We must be ready to adapt to change, to move or play a new role as circumstances require.

For example, take my grandfather. After serving in World War I, he came back and got a good job as a liquor salesman, got married, and had four kids. He lost that job when Prohibition hit, but he reinvented himself as a doll salesman while running bootleg liquor in Kentucky. (Ironically, Laurie's grandfather worked for the Bureau of Alcohol, Tobacco, and Firearms. They never met.) He later became an insurance executive and then a liquor salesman again. He was never just his job. He was adaptable, agile, and never afraid to change with the times.

Here's a mantra for emotional agility: *I'm not my job, I'm not my home, I'm not my status.*

For example, if we believe we are "our job" or our status, if we think we are "our home" or the place we live, then what happens when we lose our job, retire, have to move, or lose our status? We may feel loss, confusion about who we are, or a desire to cling to old ways; change will knock us down.

Almost by definition, being human means being adaptable and flexible. Society likes to put us in boxes — doctor, construction worker, mom, businessperson, firefighter — but we are so much more than our roles. For proof, consider people in your own family history or any famous person you admire. Their life will likely be a testament to our extraordinary ability — as individuals — to adapt and change, to remain nimble when that "something" comes at you.

Plan B Thinking

When the dragon shows up at your doorstep, the best-laid plans are often shredded.

There is a cliché that planning is indispensable, but plans are worthless. Firefighting is a perfect example of this. We start with a plan that makes sense. How to attack the fire, whether to go inside or fight it from the outside, where to get water. Sometimes it works. But sometimes the plan goes to hell in a handbasket. On some calls, there are simply not enough firefighters or equipment, or something breaks, or an engine gets stuck in the mud.

Firefighters become adept at having a "plan B," something to fall back on when the first plan is defeated by the dragon. On a complicated call, we often assign plan B thinking to a particular firefighter so we are ready the instant that plan A doesn't pan out.

To be honest, in my darker moments, after seeing so many life plans destroyed by dragons, I have wondered at the value of making plans at all. Part of me thinks that it's best just to live day by day and see what happens. But that is a pessimistic and unnatural way to live.

So we make plans, we have dreams, while knowing that those plans often will go awry — and that is just life.

Take, for example, the athlete or the dancer. To succeed, they need to be 100 percent committed to their goal. The effort it takes is often all-consuming. Yet at the same time, any injury can quickly derail a career. What then?

Thus, even when everything is going according to plan, it is a good idea to be asking the question, What if this doesn't work out? What is my plan B?

Develop a plan B (and maybe even a plan C) before things go wrong. This will help you shift gears more quickly and remain nimble. It will not alleviate the pain of having to discard your vision, if that's what you must do, but you won't spend two years not knowing what to do with the rest of your life.

Life is about change and dragons. Either we are prepared — in an athletic stance — or we are not.

There's No Such Thing as Bad Weather...

The weather is just the weather; it happens. It's been happening for millions of years and will continue for a few more million. The cycles of the seasons notwithstanding, the weather is nothing if not unpredictable, and that will only get worse with climate change.

But I like to say there's no such thing as bad weather, just unprepared people. This might seem like a rash statement, but think about it. If you live in coastal Florida, rising waters and hurricanes are a fact of life. The Midwest is "tornado alley." The West is known for wildfires.

No place is free from dangerous, unpredictable weather, so the only real question is, Are you prepared or not? If you are not ready, you risk disaster. If you are prepared, you increase the chances that you will come through — if not unscathed — at least with a better shot of surviving.

All problems in life are like this, and we are either emotionally prepared or we are not.

A firefighter knows that at any moment the pager might tone us out to a destabilizing and life-changing event. That knowledge is in our bones. We understand that we are a phone call away from an emergency. As James Baldwin says, society tries to build illusions to the contrary, but artists and firefighters (and you) know the truth. Nothing is stable, and that is the way it has been, the way it is, and the way it always will be.

The ground is shaky. It is an illusion to believe otherwise. So bend your knees, and be prepared to move in any direction.

Field Notes: On Being Prepared

1. Assume there is a dragon coming toward you. Accept deep in your psyche that everything can change in a day, that the firmament where you stand is inherently shaky. It is.

2. Know the geography of your life: What types of emergencies come with the territory?

3. Take care of the simple things: Make lists of emergency contacts, organize critical documents (like wills), plan emergency escape routes from home, establish meeting places if your family is separated.

4. Run crisis scenarios: What would you do in a house fire or medical emergency, if you lost a pet?

5. Consider "plan B" for your life: What if you lose your job? What if you change careers? What if your finances collapse? What if you have to move? How will things change if you get married, get divorced, have kids, retire? Being prepared can help.

CHAPTER FIFTEEN

STAY INSIDE THE HULA HOOP

The battlefield is a scene of constant chaos. The winner will be the one who controls that chaos, both his own and the enemies.

— NAPOLEON BONAPARTE

REEEE! "Hondo, respond to mile marker 292 southbound. Car crash, possible fatalities." There was urgency in the dispatcher's voice.

"We've gotten multiple 911s. Possible fatalities."

It was 2 AM, a Sunday morning in the summer.

I drove down our road, shaking myself awake, tucking my shirt in and stuffing medical gloves in my pocket.

At the end of our road, I parked my car and waited. I heard our rescue truck first, its sirens blaring. I got out with my flashlight and waved the truck down.

Dan was driving. I jumped in the passenger side. On the radio, the dispatcher was willing us to get there faster. She asked: "Do you want another ambulance? Do you want a helicopter? Should we dispatch mutual aid?"

Dan, his voice still full of sleep, replied curtly, "Yes."

A few minutes later, we rolled up on the scene. People were standing around — just staring — not a good sign. The scene was lit by the headlights of stopped cars. To brace myself, I pressed my hand against the ceiling of the truck as we bumped over the median of the interstate. Dan hit the floodlights. The scene became hallucinogenic: The colors were washed out by the floodlights, and everything seemed to be in black and white. The strobes from the state police car added to the effect.

On the radio, Dan announced, "Hondo Rescue on scene, chief has command. Incoming units channel four. Report to command."

We looked at the scene. There was a semitruck and a destroyed car underneath the semi. Two bodies were on the road. Dan pointed to one of the individuals.

"Patient care on that guy," he told me. "He's patient number one."

I grabbed a medical bag and jogged over. Kneeling down by the patient's head, I could see it was bad. He was young, he was unconscious, and his face was crushed. I yelled, "Hey, did anyone see how he got here?"

The crowd, numbed by what they saw, didn't answer. One older guy just shrugged.

I couldn't figure out how he got here. Was he dragged out of the car by passersby? Was he thrown out on impact? I grabbed the airway bag and took out an oral airway — the simplest of our airway tools. I repositioned his head and opened his mouth. With my hand I scooped some of the blood, goop, and broken teeth out of his mouth. I put the airway in and made sure that it was positioned right. I looked at his chest. It was also crushed. I couldn't tell if it was rising and falling. I couldn't tell if he was breathing at all. I felt for a carotid artery pulse. There was a thready, faint beat.

I took a couple of deep breaths to try to relax. I grabbed the bag valve mask, held it to his face, and started to do rescue breathing. I squeezed the bag. To my horror, blood and air bubbled out from the orbits of his eyes. His face was one massive series of fractures.

"Shit," I whispered to myself.

I called to Dan. "Dan, I need help!"

He turned to me and shook his head, "Can't help. I'll send you the next medic that shows up." He turned back to study the entire scene.

I put my head down close to this boy's head and listened for any sounds of breathing and felt again for a carotid pulse.

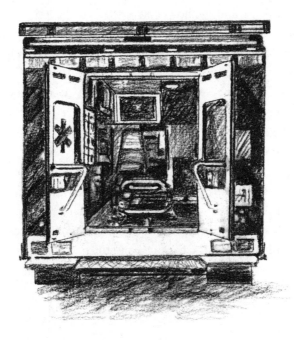

Now there was nothing. I started CPR. I cut off his shirt, found the midline of his chest, and leaned over him. I locked my elbows, made sure my hands were in the right position, and began compressions.

Finally, our ambulance and extra hands showed up. Adrenalized, I said, "Let's scoop and run." We put him on a backboard. His arms and head flopped over the side.

"One, two, three, lift," I said to the crew. We lifted the board and our patient onto the gurney and slid the gurney into the ambulance. The last thing I saw was the kid's arm hanging down off the gurney. The EMT slammed the door, and the ambulance screamed into the night, down the interstate to the hospital.

Within minutes, the second patient, another teenager, was loaded in the second ambulance, and it also flew toward the city lights and the hospital.

Then we were done. I rocked back and sat on my heels. I took off my gloves, caked in blood, and tossed them in the wreckage of the car.

We knew they were both gone, both dead. They had slipped our grasp like a man on a cliff letting go and falling into the darkness.

A few minutes later, everyone was gone except our rescue truck and the state police. We were in a small pool of light; floodlights, flashing red lights, and strobes. I looked up into the vault of the New Mexico night. It was dark and clear. The Milky Way was a wild paintbrush stroke of colors across the sky. But I could feel the darkness and the implacability of the universe pressing down on us. Like every firefighter I knew, I prayed for a moment that the universe, or the spirits, would gently embrace these two little ones and care for them.

Assessing a Bad Call:
Order and Stillness within Chaos

After a bad call like this, when there are fatalities, we usually gather together the next day to discuss what happened — what we did and what we could've done better. It's difficult because the emotions are often raw, but it's important to help us learn and get ready for the next bad call.

If you were in the station with us, you might ask why Dan refused to help me.

The reason is simple and part of our discipline. In emergency scenes, within the chaotic first few minutes, we've learned someone must stay as "command" and not get sucked in. Without a command presence, a difficult call can go down the tubes quickly. In incident command school, they practice this by simulating scenes. They make the "incident commander" stand inside a hula hoop and stay there, no matter who is yelling at them or crying for help.

The goal is for the incident commander to see the big picture, the entire scene, and be able to make often difficult decisions, like who goes in which ambulance and when.

It sounds simple, but in practice it can be hard. There are dozens of pulls on your attention: Other firefighters are requesting assignments; the radio is blaring; witnesses, passersby, patients, and victims are clamoring for your attention. Emotions run high and many voices can be edged with panic.

The opposite of standing in the hula hoop and seeing the big picture is called tunnel vision. I had tunnel vision. I was focused on the patient dying in front of me. That was my assignment, and I had no idea what was going on with the rest of the scene. Tunnel vision is a double-edged sword. On the one hand, you need to be highly focused sometimes, but on the other, you don't want to lose sight of the big picture. You don't want to be treating a patient on the highway and belatedly discover there is no traffic control as cars whiz by you.

Another thing that can happen when things fall apart on an emergency scene is that responders begin to "freelance." They run to the loudest patient or take a hose line off an engine and start spraying water without a plan or without checking in with command. This often causes more chaos than it helps.

Once at a fire, two different fire departments showed up, they didn't establish a command structure (no one was standing in the hula hoop), and they both began attacking the fire from different sides of the building using different strategies. The house burned down. It might have anyway — house fires can be like that — but having two uncoordinated departments going at it didn't help.

In any emergency, our first task, other than to immediately save lives, is to reduce the chaos. Emergencies are disrupters; they explode our day-to-day routines; they often cause pain that feels untreatable and a sense that nothing will be normal again. When these moments happen in your life, it is important to think about imposing order. During the first minutes of a crisis, stay inside the hula hoop and coordinate the scene. Avoid tunnel vision; don't just run off to the loudest person or treat the problem that is right at your feet.

There is a larger point here. Oddly, that vision of Dan standing still while people were running, trucks were arriving, and firefighters were clamoring for orders has stuck with me ever since. I think of it this way: We are currently living our lives at warp speed. We are busier and more inundated with information than at any time I can recall. Every day can feel like a crisis.

Ironically, bad calls like this one — after hundreds of times driving an ambulance with strobes piercing the darkness and sirens blaring at 2 AM — have made me want to step back, stop, and be still.

All those individuals who have passed through our hands, their plans and lives interrupted, have made me want to be, if just for a moment, still. Increasingly, I just want to stop for a moment and understand the bigger picture.

We can't understand the bigger picture when we are moving so fast that we can barely complete a thought.

T. S. Eliot wrote, "At the still point of the turning world. Neither flesh nor fleshless; Neither from nor towards; at the still point, there the dance is."

I don't care whether you are Buddhist, Christian, atheist, or a rider of the purple sage. Be you a cleric, a banker, or both, it makes no difference. We can find the moments to be still no matter how chaotic our world or how fast the current is flowing.

We can be still, listen to our hearts beat, and wonder at all of this — this life we are living.

We can emulate Dan standing at that scene, still and staring, intently trying to understand. We can be still, can find the still point, and ask those big, profound questions: What's going on? How do I fit in? What are we to do?

Be still for a moment and find that mythical hula hoop. Let the chaos sweep by you but not into you.

That is how you figure things out.
That is how you see your own big picture.
That is where the dance is.
Be still.

Field Notes: Stay Inside the Hula Hoop

In the fire service, when we respond to difficult calls, when it is a crisis, we have "field guides" with prompts to help us remember what to do and what actions to take. Here is a version of that for when we run into a crisis. Stay inside the hula hoop and ask these questions:

1. Are you physically safe and will you be able to stay safe? (We first always ask, "Is the scene secure?")
2. Does someone need to be "rescued" right now? Is someone physically or emotionally in harm's way, and they need to be removed from the situation immediately?
3. What is the big picture? We do a "360," a complete walk around a burning structure or a car crash so that we see and understand the entire situation. We don't want to miss anything; we want the most comprehensive understanding of the problem that we can get as soon as possible. For us that means staying inside the hula hoop and assuring that we understand the problem before taking action. Think first, ask questions second, then act.
4. What help is needed? Is this a simple problem that you can handle by yourself or is it a "four-alarm fire," where you need lots of help and need it quickly?

What kind of help do you need? Medical? Legal? Family? Friends?

5. How much time do you have? There are two types of emergencies. Those where we need to act quickly to save life and limb or those where we take our time, keep everyone safe, and figure out the best solutions.

CHAPTER SIXTEEN

GET UNDER THE SMOKE

The more clearly we see the reality of the world,
the better equipped we are to deal with the world.

— M. SCOTT PECK, *The Road Less Traveled*

Imagine this: You're a firefighter. You've come to a home
that is burning. Deep inside the house a dragon is nesting
and cooking away.

Your team bunkers up, puts on their SCBAs and masks,
and checks their radios. You turn your air on, and your
breathing sounds like Darth Vader, a deep *keesh-whoosh*. An
officer checks your gear, making sure that you have no exposed skin and that you are "buttoned up."

Another firefighter opens the door, and smoke billows
out. You can feel the heat pulsate from the interior. As you
walk in, hauling the hose line, you're enveloped in smoke and
heat. You can't see, and the temperature climbs as you move
toward the seat of the fire.

So you drop to your knees. Immediately, even through
your bunker gear, you notice that it is cooler close to the floor
and, under the smoke, you can see. Crawling, pushing the

hose line forward, you turn the corner into a bedroom. There, in the corner, is the fire billowing up the wall. You open your nozzle and with a straight stream aim at the seat of the fire. A few seconds and the smoke in the room turns from black to gray, then white. A few more hits from the hose and the fire is knocked down, and the air starts to clear. A child's room appears, full of smoke and still hot, but decorated in the stuff of childhood.

When we fight an interior fire, we get underneath the smoke and the heat so that we can see, so we can understand what we're facing. We need that clarity.

Today, technology has given us a big boost. We have thermal imaging cameras that can see the fire through the smoke and see heat and fire through walls and ceiling. This is all a quest for clarity: Where is the dragon, how big is it, and where is it moving?

On a call with an older woman in pain, it is the same quest. We ask questions: Where is the pain? What kind of pain? How bad? How long have you had it? Does anything help? Have you had it before? We seek clarity to understand what we're facing and how we can help. On one particular call, our questions led us to cancer and to the concern that the woman's daughter was stealing her pain meds, her Oxy-Contin.

Confusion is the handmaiden of emergencies. It takes time, energy, and focus to clear the smoke and get answers. The firefighter life is all about getting under the smoke, both the actual smoke of a fire and the smoke and heat of chaos and panic, so that we can see clearly.

Without clarity, we make assumptions and jump to conclusions.

In any emergency, any crisis, it is the same. In the beginning, there is confusion, smoke, too many questions, and not enough answers.

In a crisis, we are like the firefighter enveloped in smoke trying to find the clear air underneath.

Cut Through the Smoke by Asking Questions

When we arrive at a fire, our first task is to get as much information as possible, to cut through the smoke and find the important facts. This is another reason why, during our response to the accident in the last chapter, Dan, the incident commander, stayed inside the "hula hoop": He needed to get under the smoke of chaos to understand what had happened.

It took a minute or so to reconstruct the crash: The boys had not seen a semitruck moving slowly up the interstate in the dark, and they had plowed into it at high speed. Their car was underneath the truck and destroyed. Our next question was: How many patients were in the car? None of the bystanders knew, and we couldn't make assumptions. Once the two patients had been loaded into ambulances and sent to the hospital, we did a search for others.

We weren't going to leave the scene until we had the clearest picture we could get of what had happened, and we had done everything we could possibly do.

In the midst of an active emergency, it is not uncommon for the most well-intended individuals to have complicated stories to tell and to be too upset to explain clearly. There is the smoke of confusion and chaos, and the task is to quickly cut through to find the facts, to figure out what is important and what is not.

The same is true in any emergency, when any crisis is complicated and "smoky" with panic and fear. Someone needs to stand in the hula hoop and be the smoke cutter, asking the important questions to find clarity.

When my younger sister, Susie, was dying of cancer, she fell into a coma, and my other sister and I weren't sure what was happening or what to do. The physician's assistant assigned to her sat us down and patiently and in simple language explained Susie's disease. She wrote the name of the disease on the whiteboard, leptomeningeal carcinomatosis, which is a cancer of the lining around the brain. It is fatal 95 percent of the time with a prognosis of four to six weeks. The PA patiently sat with us, talked about options, answered our questions, and then told us to call her if we ever had more questions. She was our advocate that morning, our smoke cutter.

Sometimes, we'd rather not get under the smoke to understand the nature of a crisis. Sometimes the truth sucks. And sometimes the truth is genuinely complicated, with few definitive or satisfying answers.

The Elusiveness of the Truth

It often takes a lot of digging to get the truth. Opinions and assumptions often obscure hard and real truths. But sometimes what's true is beyond our grasp. More than occasionally, just when we think we've discovered the truth about something, we get under the smoke and find this truth is an illusion.

Once, we were paged to an assault. Our patient was a seventeen-year-old female who had been beaten by her boyfriend with a steel pipe. Luckily, she was alert and conscious with just bruises. We were, of course, outraged and righteous as the sheriff walked the boy in cuffs to the squad car.

As we took the young girl's history, we discovered that she had been kicked out of her home, been on heroin, been clean, found a boyfriend, and found work. The relationship with the boyfriend was abusive with a history of calls to law enforcement. Then the girl mused that most of the time she was the one attacking her boyfriend. She shrugged and said she'd been diagnosed with "intermittent rage disorder," and she would become violent out of the blue. At this point, my partner, David, slowly and discreetly removed the scalpel that was taped to the wall of the ambulance.

Writ large, of course, we are all continually trying to get under the smoke, cut through complexity, and grasp the truth about ourselves. We have moments of clarity, both large and small, both disturbing and enlightening.

Those moments of clarity often resonate around big questions.

Why am I here? Who am I? Who do I love? Am I loved? Why do I do what I do? What do I stand for?

Those moments of clarity are often caused by crisis. A divorce, losing a job, losing parents, getting seriously ill — these events can prompt us to get under the smoke by asking big questions. Like the dragon fire in the corner of the room, certain problems glower at us, demanding answers.

Crisis begets pain. But crisis often brings clarity.

This is why I believe we need to always dedicate ourselves to getting under the smoke, finding the clear air so that we can see. It is not easy. Crawling into a dark and smoky structure takes courage. But it is how we fight fires. It is the path to clarity: Get under the smoke.

Field Notes: Under the Smoke

Every true emergency is obscured by the smoke of confusion, sometimes panic, and lots of opinions. The smoke can be the chaos of an emergency or of a complicated medical diagnosis.

The goal of getting under the smoke is to seek clarity by asking the following questions:

1. What is the "smoke"? What elements obscure us from seeing the problem clearly or are causing confusion?
2. What assumptions do we hold? What are we "making up" that might not be true?
3. What facts are known? What questions should be asked?
4. What are priorities, and what are not priorities?
5. Who is in the best position, physically and emotionally, to be the "smoke cutter," someone who can objectively find and deal with the facts of the situation?

CHAPTER SEVENTEEN

THE DRAGON FIRE

Life is suffering.

— BUDDHA

It took me a second to remember what the screeching sound was; it was 4 AM, and Laurie and I were both deep asleep. A few seconds passed before I finally remembered: *Our pagers, fire department, get up!*

"Hey," I said, coming to my senses, "I think it's a fire."

"God," Laurie replied, peeking out the window at the moonless night.

We jumped out of bed, disoriented, still sleepy, but soon we were dressed and driving.

This was our fifth month on the department and our first fire. It was also one of the last times that Laurie and I would respond together in the middle of the night. The day before we had just found out that she was pregnant with our first child. Laurie planned to continue to go on calls as long as she felt comfortable. After the baby was born, we realized that we'd be flipping a lot of coins to see who'd respond and who would stay home.

Knowing that we were going to our first real fire woke us up as we drove down our road. On the fire department radio, the chief told us all the department trucks had responded and we should come directly to the fire in our car. A few minutes on the interstate and we saw the orange glow. Turning onto the street, I opened my window. I could smell smoke and a sweetly sickening odor inside the smoke, and soon the full scene came into view.

"Wow!" Laurie whispered as we walked up the driveway, buckling our bunker coats.

It was a big fire; the house was already fully involved. Fires are a game of time. It takes only minutes for a small fire in one room to explode into a catastrophic house fire. A house fire can double in size each minute. By appearances, this fire had been burning for a while. In rural areas like ours, by the time we get the page, respond, and arrive at the fire, it can be fifteen to twenty minutes. By then it can be too late to save the house.

Fire attacks all your senses. You feel, smell, hear, taste, and see it.

Fire is a living thing. You watch it dance as walls and roofs collapse, flames leaping thirty feet in the night sky, radiating a heat so intense that it makes you turn away. It crouches in the corner of a room, dark red and glowering, shrouded in black smoke, whispering to you, *Break a window, open a door, and let me suck the air out of the universe.* You feel terror when its flames turn and bend toward you in tall grass. It wants to see you run, knowing you're no match: It will catch you.

Fire will burn until there is no more fuel. It will not stop; it will not tire. Give it fuel, and it will grow. It will devour houses, forests, and neighborhoods. Fire can eat them all.

Fire is the destroyer. This is the reason we have fire departments, not just "emergency" departments. Fire is the real and mortal enemy. Deep in our ancestral DNA lies the terror of this dragon.

But this early morning, barely awake and at our first fire, we were not thinking anything this metaphorical. We were simply praying not to do something stupid.

We walked up to our chief, Dan. He was standing by his old Bronco, on the radio, silhouetted by flames. There was the sucking sound of air flowing into heat. Smoke was dark and rolling out of the windows.

Firefighters were yelling, hauling hoses off the engine, and setting up water tanks. Three firefighters were throwing on SCBAs. In their helmets and masks, they looked like medieval knights. Every few seconds they turned around and sized up the fire. They didn't look scared, just excited.

"What do you need?" Laurie shouted to Dan over the roar.

The radio crackled. "Command, everyone is out of the house except the dogs. Owner says there are twenty-three dogs. Most still inside."

Dan looked at the assistant chief, Paul. Paul just shook his head.

"She was an animal hoarder," Paul turned to us and said. "The house is full of dogs. But when we got here all the doors were locked. The fire was everywhere. The dogs never had a chance. Most of them are piled up by the back door. I saw them when we did our first walk-around."

"Jesus," Laurie whispered.

I shook my head. That was the sickly-sweet smell, all those dogs...

Dan got back on the radio. "Let's pull back. Exterior attack only."

He looked at the house. Flames had breached the roof, and it was collapsing. The windows had blown out. Heavy smoke poured from every crevice.

Paul shrugged. "It's lost. No one goes in, too dangerous. Even if there were people in there, it's too late. We couldn't save them."

"We have enough folks up here," Dan told us. "Go move that supply line to the side of the driveway so we can get the city engine up here."

Laurie and I looked at each other, knowing we'd never get over the smell. We turned and headed down. Thirty yards away, I could still feel the heat on my back.

The big yellow supply line snaked down the driveway. We got down on our knees and shoved. It took us a few minutes of muddy struggle, but we finally pushed it to the side. As soon as we were done, another engine roared by us to join the attack. As we followed it back, one of my boots got stuck in the caliche mud. I yanked it out and limped — boot half on — the rest of the way back to command.

Paul told us to stand by. The early excitement of a big fire had drained out of everyone. The two engines had hose lines out, and firefighters were flooding the structure with water.

Thirty minutes later, the fire was extinguished. The dogs were dead, and with the house gone, their remains were visible through the smoke.

Dan was sitting on the hood of his truck, his bunkers and white helmet caked with grime. The eastern sky was starting to brighten. Crews were walking through the skeleton of the house putting out hot spots. I heard a woman's voice yell, "Damn!" Then, "I'm fine, I just stepped on a dead dog. They're everywhere!"

Laurie and I drained and stacked hoses and collected equipment.

In the end, Dan came up to us. Laurie was sitting on the back of the ambulance. I was leaning on a shovel. We smelled like smoke. My bunkers were now dirty, and Laurie's face was smudged with soot.

"God," Laurie said, "all those dogs. I never heard any barking; they must have all lost consciousness from the smoke before they died."

Dan nodded. "Yep, it's awful."

"Well," I said, "at least a couple got out. I saw them running around the scene. They must be terrified."

Dan took off his helmet and threw it in his truck. "I called animal control. They'll round up the strays and take them to the shelter. That's about all we can do."

Laurie whispered, "This sucks."

"Ya," Dan replied. "But we did everything we could."

Laurie looked at the shell of the house.

The Conversation

Dan continued, "You can't care too much. You have to stay detached. Otherwise, you won't last in the department. Other people have the luxury of getting upset, but if we get too emotional about it, we won't be able to do the work."

He pointed to the distraught owner. Pain emanated from her in waves as she talked to the police.

We stood in a little group, fatigue settling in and the eastern sky becoming day.

At the core of this conversation was the assumption that if we allow in the suffering of others, we will also suffer and feel pain. It's the worry that, over time, suffering will erode us. We think we have a quota for suffering, and if we exceed it, we will not emotionally survive.

Thus we are taught as firefighters that you can't care too much. You need to keep your distance, you can't get emotional.

At the same time, you don't want to become so callous, so detached, that you lose touch with why you became a firefighter.

It can be a hard needle to thread, a balancing act.

I've seen the gamut and run the gamut, from being completely detached and uncaring to being neutral, empathic, vulnerable, and open-hearted.

Where I've landed is simple. I strive to be open-hearted, to not run from suffering, but to embrace it.

I say "strive to be" because it can be difficult in the face of the same kinds of calls. Firefighters see the same crashes, the breathing problems, the drug overdoses, and the fires. It's difficult not to become attenuated, to not even name the patient, but instead name the disease: "eighteen-year-old male overdose."

I say "strive to be" because it is natural to build a wall between ourselves and suffering, between our comfortable world and that of the patient or victim.

The theologian Martin Buber wrote that we can see the world and people through the lens of "I-it," where others are just objects, or we can see the world through the lens of "I-thou," where others are full humans beings — just like us. It is a profound shift in perspective.

Or as another firefighter once told me (more simply than Buber): "When I go to an overdose and think of it as just another addict, I feel pissed off and like I'm wasting my time. But when I think of the patient as just like me, and I'm helping them, then I feel like I'm making a difference, even if it is a small one. It makes me feel good about myself."

So I suggest this path, both for firefighters and for anyone subject to the human condition. Embrace suffering; don't run from it or become callous to it. The pain of others will make you uncomfortable, but it will not kill you. It will change you. But the change will be toward a more compassionate and less judgmental self. Yes, there are risks. Dan was right — the wrong set of calls, the bad calls, the true tragedies take a toll: We each have a quota of what we can handle.

But the paradox is that embracing suffering is the path to becoming a full human being.

The truth of the matter is this. Not everyone has their house burn down. But we all suffer in ways unique to us. We don't get out of this life without suffering. So let us learn to accept suffering, ours and that of others, as part of the whole, as part of the human experience. As firefighters, our job is to run not just toward the burning building but toward suffering. Maybe that is everyone's task: to see the homeless vet, to see the drug addict, to see the house fire, and recognize the universality of suffering. Maybe the task is to allow that kind of pain in and see what happens.

At another fire where we actually saved the house, defeated the dragon, I listened to a firefighter run toward the suffering. He consoled the owner, the mom. He didn't have to; we'd put the fire out, done our job, and felt like celebrating. But he listened intently to the mom describe how this was the home they had built for their family, that all her kids were grown up and gone, but it was still the family home, now damaged. He just listened to her pain. Afterward, he told me that he thought it was part of the job — part of the work — not only to deal with fire but to remember that there are individuals affected, people whose lives are changed, and his job was to be there for them.

"What," he told me, "if it was my mom, my family who had nearly lost our home? That is how I want to think and show up."

Simply, in the land of dragons, where suffering happens, we need to know how to support — and not run from — the suffering of others.

Let me end with a story my father told me about a legendary friend of his, the psychiatrist Dr. Otis Maxfield. My dad had a meeting with him once at the hospital. In the middle of the meeting, Dr. Maxfield excused himself, got up, and walked over to two orderlies standing on either side of a woman. The woman was dressed in a loose hospital gown, half-naked, wearing slippers. She was obese, angry, swearing at the top of her lungs, spitting. She was the archetype of someone most of us automatically avoid. The orderlies were at the end of their patience.

My dad said Dr. Maxfield walked right up to her, opened his arms, and hugged her, asking, "How are you doing, Helen?" And she smiled. A small thing. But it's another model of how to act: See suffering. Embrace it. Don't run from it.

CHAPTER EIGHTEEN

WE ARE NOT SUPERHEROES

They chose to do it because it was difficult.

— MARY DORIA RUSSELL, *The Sparrow*

REEEE! "Hondo, car versus motorcycle. Mile marker 295." Greg and I arrived on scene at the same time. Again chaos: cars and trucks everywhere. Another interstate parking lot.

We walked up the last twenty yards. Dan and Sheila pulled up right behind us in the rescue truck. Dan got out and elevated the big light tower. He turned the lights on and turned night into a black-and-white movie.

What we saw was horrible. There was a destroyed motorcycle and body parts.

Greg and I were standing next to each other.

"Fuck," I said.

I looked at Greg. "You take patient care? I'll take triage?"

Greg, an ex-combat paramedic, had seen this before.

"Got it." He nodded and walked over to the first patient, a guy down on the road, missing a leg.

He immediately turned to me and yelled, "Scoop and run!"

Our code to go fast. Use the backboard like a spatula, slide the unconscious patient on it, and go. Patient care would be done at eighty miles an hour.

Greg yelled to Dan as they were loading, "Dan, see if you can find this guy's leg!" — he pointed — "By the pickup!"

Dan jogged over to the truck. I saw him kneel down, reach under the truck, and pull out, not a full leg, just shredded bone and flesh.

Dan carried it to the ambulance. Greg shook his head, but they put what remained of the leg on the board. Then the doors shut, and they were off, weaving through stalled traffic.

I saw another pair of legs underneath a semitractor. A medic came behind, and I pointed him toward that patient.

He looked under the truck and back out quickly. He turned to me and shook his head. She was dead, decapitated.

"Holy Christ," he said.

He walked away to get a blanket to cover her. The ambulance with our first patient was now in the distance, strobes flashing, heading up the other side of the valley to the hospital. I could hear the siren wailing up the hill.

Again, just like that, it was over. Standing in a small group, we pieced it together. They'd been on the motorcycle. The interstate narrowed going through the pass, and at seventy-five miles an hour, they clipped a stalled pickup truck. The stalled truck ripped the man's leg off and tossed him. The bike slid, and they were immediately run over by a semi, killing the woman.

A state police officer interrupted us, "Hey, that light tower is great. Can you stay and keep the scene lit? That would really help."

Dan nodded. He looked at us and rolled his eyes. This

was one of the unintended consequences of the rescue truck he had designed. Cops loved it for night work.

The scene was now an investigation, the long and detailed evidence-gathering time. It can take hours for the "fatality teams" to film, measure, and search for clues. Grim work.

I was assigned traffic. I walked down the line of stopped vehicles on the midnight interstate to let them know that it was going to be a while. There was a woman with a Chihuahua on her lap driving a big FedEx truck. She just nodded; she'd seen it all. A taciturn Hispanic cowboy in a pickup stared straight ahead, said nothing. A family, kids in the back, drinking coke, playing computer games, mom zonked out, dad resting his head on the steering wheel. The dad waved his hand at me. Another family pulling a trailer with all their belongs, a modern-day *Grapes of Wrath* story, little ones asleep; mom, the driver, pissed off at me for telling her that it might be an hour before we opened a lane. A woman in a Lexus with Tennessee plates, her face streaked with tears, wiped her eyes with her jacket sleeve when I knocked on her window. I didn't ask why she was crying.

Two more hours passed. Then the state police released the fire department. I got in my car and headed home. I drove down into the Cañoncito Valley and up the other side. In my rearview mirror, I saw the bright light of the rescue-truck tower illuminating the road. I got on the radio.

"You're going to be there all night," I said to Dan.

"Yeah. Sucks. But I drove rescue. Sheila took Engine One back to the station. So I'm stuck with it."

"Call me if you want me to replace you."

"Sure. Rescue out."

I went home.

See how strange it is? This call didn't affect me. It's just how it goes. The call with the mom in the river devastated me, and a few years before this call, I had passed out in the ER while I was bagging a six-year-old trauma patient. But this call didn't get to me.

I went to bed. The next morning, Jed, our chief, called me.

"Dan quit. He's done."

"What?" I asked. "What happened?"

"He turned his gear in this morning. You should talk to him."

Jed hung up. I stared out into space.

Here is how Hondo volunteer firefighters — with twenty-five years in — retire. On the appointed day they drop their gear off at Station One. They stack their gear in the meeting room. Boots with the pants over them, suspenders through the bootstraps. Jacket folded neatly over the boots and their helmet on top. That's what Dan did that morning. He was done.

That night I went over to his house. We grabbed a couple of beers. His wife, Patty, and the kids had mysteriously disappeared.

We talked about football. We talked about the department.

We were sitting in their kitchen, light pouring in from the setting sun.

"So," I asked. "You're done?"

Dan took a sip of beer. "Jed call you?"

I nodded, drank some beer.

"Figures. Yep, last night was it for me. I was out there, sitting in rescue, moving up the road inch by inch so they could videotape the scene. I couldn't stop thinking."

He laughed, and said, "I know I always told you not to think. But last night…"

Dan drank his beer. Put the bottle down on the kitchen counter.

"Anyway, they had a chalk outline of her body, just like in the old movies. I was just staring at it. I saw some of her flesh still stuck in the pavement."

"Maybe we should switch to rum," I said.

"Ha, probably." He laughed. "I'm not going to sleep tonight. Anyway, all those boxes — where I lock up the bad calls in my mind — flooded open, all the questions that I never wanted to hear or ask."

He finished his beer.

"I wondered who she was. I thought of her as a baby girl, then a girl like our kids. You know, she was the love of her parents."

He stopped for a minute, looked out at the setting sun.

"She had hopes, dreams, and boyfriends.... And it ended right there on I-25 in fucking Cañoncito, New Mexico, in the middle of the night."

"Jesus," I said. "Some of us shoulda stuck around."

He shrugged. "It wouldn't have made any difference. I just knew I'd seen too much of this, I've been doing it too long, and it was late. Really late. I knew I was done. I had no more boxes to fill."

We sat for a while. It was quiet. The sun went down.

Dan continued, "After we were done, about 3:30, I drove rescue back to the station, put my gear by the door, called Jed, and told him. Bingo. Over."

I got up, went to their bar, and made two rum and tonics. I handed one to Dan.

"Here's to no pagers," I said.

He nodded. "Yep."

We sat and talked and drank until eleven. Until we were both silent.

I had a lot to drink that night, so Laurie came and picked me up.

I wondered about Dan. He was an iconic firefighter who was on the department for twenty-five years. A thousand times, he was the guy we looked up to. He'd been the most committed and fearless firefighter I have ever worked with. I thought him invulnerable.

I grew up, and maybe you did, too, with the idea that being emotionally invulnerable was a good thing, something you needed to become as an adult, as a man.

For a firefighter, this means that calls don't get to you, or if they do, it's temporary, something that passes. There is nothing out there, we think, that will make us quit, mess us up, or stress us out to the point where we can't function.

Being a firefighter has taught me this is laughable and another illusion. It sets you up for a true fall from grace. The truth is that we are vulnerable and fallible human beings, each one of us. For firefighters, there is a call out there, or a series of calls, that will get to you, that will make you turn in your gear. No firefighter is exempt.

Neither, by the way, is anyone else. There is always something out there that will pierce the thickest walls, the most robust defense. There are calls out there that will test you, make you want to pass out, run, or throw up your hands and say, "I can't handle this."

Superheroes are fiction. The trick is to accept the fact that we are vulnerable, to accept the fact that we might not act the way we want to act in a crisis, to accept the fact that we don't have all the answers, that we are in fact fallible. Even for firefighters — who train and train, and who experience all sorts of trauma and suffering — there are limits.

Knowing this, that we have limits, that we are not superheroes, is actually empowering. Do we have to be tough sometimes? Yes. Do we need thick skins occasionally? Of course. Life is difficult, hard.

But we can expend so much energy trying to be the toughest, the smartest, the most impenetrable person in the room. We spend so much energy that it is exhausting.

A better strategy is to let go of the superhero ideology. A better strategy is to think, *I'm going to show up. I'm going to practice compassion, do the best I can, and accept that I might fail, I might falter. But I will show up.*

That to me is the most authentic stance. That is the best we can do.

part four

THE GRIEF ROAD

The deeper that sorrow carves
into your being, the more joy
you can contain.

— KAHLIL GIBRAN, *The Prophet*

Firefighters experience life condensed. Packed into a career, even a short one, are all the passions and sorrows of living. If you're attuned as a firefighter, the human experience flows through you; births, pain, joy, suffering, and death.

That is the palette.

Now we come to the next color on our palette, and that is grief. When Laurie and I joined the fire service, we understood there would be tough calls. But we didn't consider the idea that we would become familiar with the cycles of grief. When we signed on, there wasn't a clause in the paperwork that said: "Be aware there will be calls, a half dozen, that will defeat all your defenses."

The first lesson I learned was that grieving is personal, different for each of us. It doesn't follow a set of steps. The second lesson learned was that the same event can cause different reactions, an astonishing variety of individual responses. Finally and importantly, I learned we should not judge ourselves — or others — on how we respond, on how grieving shows up in us.

Since grieving is personal, different for each of us, I can

only walk through my own process of grieving. Yet grief is a well-traveled road, and I hope my experience can illuminate a path for you. Hopefully, I can help make it a less painful, strange, lonely journey.

CHAPTER NINETEEN

THE MIDNIGHT CALL

Nothing good happens after midnight.

— BARBARA WOLFF, El Dorado Fire Department

Where we live, it's still possible to stop in the middle of a rural road and have a conversation with someone in another car. Two cars stopped facing opposite directions. Windows open. Talking about soccer, talking about the structure fire last week. A small town is where you wave to everyone as you drive. There is the full-hand wave, and there is the two-fingers-off-the-steering-wheel wave.

I loved raising kids in a small town. I got to know the friends of my kids and their expanded circle of friends. In a small town, you have running jokes. "Let me know when you start driving," I always told the sixteen-year-olds, "so I can stay off the roads."

"So," I'd joke with the eighteen-year-olds, stressed about their SAT scores, "I heard you got accepted to Bob's College and Auto Repair."

They would roll their eyes. My kids would tell me to cut it out.

That's how it goes in a small town. Everyone, it seems, knows everyone.

Everyone assumes we're safe. Our kids are safe. They can grow, learn, laugh, and fall in love, all with family and friends close.

This story is a midnight tale. It was a June night. Warm. The schools were finished for the year. Kids were out, enjoying their freedom.

"Hondo, Med 80, car crash. Head-on. Possible fatalities, entrapment. Old Las Vegas Highway."

I woke up, jumped out of bed, stepped over the dogs, and walked toward the garage.

Laurie and our daughters — summer night owls all — were still up, watching TV.

"Car crash," I mumbled, trying to wake up as I walked past them.

Putting my bunker pants on in the garage, I heard the ambulance responding.

I was still sleepy as I opened the garage and drove out.

Turning onto the frontage road, I heard a paramedic on the radio asking for another ambulance to respond and for the helicopter to launch. Then, over the radio, "Med 80 is on scene, two vehicles, head-on."

Then nothing.

Long before I was ready, I pulled up at the scene. There were dozens of high school kids milling around and four or five cars scattered around the scene, two of them demolished.

I got out, still trying to figure out what the hell had happened.

Looking at the kids, I yelled, "Everyone who can walk come to me and sit down on the side of the road now!"

It's how we triage a crowded scene. If you can walk and follow commands, you're okay. Some began to move. Others were still staring at the wrecked cars. I yelled it again louder.

A male voice responded, "You don't have to be so mean."

They all came and sat down in a row like they were in school.

I jogged over to the first car. Two paramedics were furiously working on a teenager, seriously injured but alive, in the driver's seat. I asked, "What do you need?" One medic shook his head and said, "The other four are all dead. We need to get this one out."

"I'll take command," I said, and the medic nodded.

I went back to my truck, closed the door, closed the window, and got on the radio.

"Incoming units, Hondo 37 has command. Command is on the south side of the crash. We have possibly three vehicles involved. Let's expedite our response. Multiple patients. Fatalities. Extrication needed. Let's close the road both directions."

I asked dispatch to page out our neighboring fire department, El Dorado.

Mike, a veteran firefighter and former chief, walked over to my car, zipping up his bunker coat.

I asked him, "Can you take operations?"

He nodded and walked to our rescue truck. He would lead our extrication.

On the radio, I asked for a landing zone crew for the helicopter.

I looked over, and the kids were still sitting in a row. Waiting.

I heard a knock on my window. It was Barbara, a paramedic from El Dorado.

I rolled down my window.

"Barb, can you take triage? Look at the car with the kids first, okay? Confirm that the four passengers are fatalities."

Barb nodded and walked over to the little car.

More firefighters checked in for assignments: extrication team, traffic, manage the kids, ready the helicopter landing zone.

Barbara came back after a few minutes and shook her head.

"They are all gone," she whispered. "All fatals."

We looked at the kids sitting on the road. We were both thinking that they didn't need to watch the rest of this unfold.

Barbara said, "Let's see if we can get all these kids out of here. Maybe we can shuttle them down to Station Two in our ambulance. The police are going to want to interview everyone."

I nodded, and she went off to do that.

The teen driver, our first and most critical patient, was loaded into the first ambulance and rushed to Station Two, about half a mile away, where we had set up an off-scene landing zone for the helicopter; from there, they would fly to the trauma center in Albuquerque. The Santa Fe ambulance reported that they were transporting another injured patient, the Jeep driver, to St. Vincent's hospital in Santa Fe.

I got out of my car and gathered together our department in a tight group. The road was covered with glass and metal. The first few minutes of chaos were over. Now we had to slow down.

I asked, "Have we located everyone?"

Mike replied, "Six total. Five in the car, which had four

fatalities, one transported by helicopter. The Jeep driver was transported to St. Vincent's. But one of the bystanders said there was someone else in the car. If so, we haven't found him yet."

"Let's search," I said.

We split up and searched with flashlights around the scene, in the brush up and down the road. We found no one.

We gathered again. Dispatch called on the radio for an update. I told them to stand by.

Time to get under the smoke. Three of us stood beneath the lights of our rescue truck and starting doing our math. Two cars involved. None of the other vehicles on the scene had any damage that we could see.

We wanted to make sure our numbers matched, that we weren't missing someone. We went through it again. I called Barbara at Station Two to verify none of the teen bystanders she'd taken there were patients.

"No," she replied. "Everyone at Station Two is fine. And our head count is confirmed."

We had accounted for everyone.

The adrenaline began to drain out of us. We waited. We wondered, *What the hell happened?* Someone said the Jeep driver had been drinking, on the wrong side of the road, and plowed into the kids. But it was hard to tell from the skid marks and from where the cars had ended up.

Mike turned to the state police officer. "Can we cover the car with sheets?" he asked.

The officer nodded.

For the next few hours, the police did their investigation, and we waited for the medical investigator to come and do their report.

Tom, our new chief, came back from the helicopter landing zone. We switched roles: he took command, and I was happy to go back to just being a firefighter.

As we waited, individuals would drift over to the car and adjust the sheets that had slipped. We covered the dead to protect their privacy in this final, most terrible, and intimate of moments. We covered them because as we started to slow down and think, seeing them was just too hard. We covered them because it's just what we do.

We waited. We cleaned and replaced the tools and equipment. We talked about the extrication yet to come, removing the dead kids from the destroyed car.

I asked Tom, "Why don't we send some guys home? We don't need everyone here. If we need them later, we can page them out."

He nodded, and I continued, "Let's just keep the old guys, okay? This is going to be too hard on some of the new folks."

Tom began sending people home.

I walked up to one of our younger guys, a college student who was standing, staring at the car. He shook his head like he was coming out of a trance.

He said, "Shit, I gotta call my girlfriend. I think I know these guys."

We cut him loose from the scene.

Mike leaned into me. "We'll have to call him later to make sure he's okay."

I nodded, and we waited. Our final job that night would be to cut the doors off the car and remove the kids. We talked about a plan.

Another young firefighter came up to me. "Look, I can

help with the tools, but I don't think I can deal with the bodies."

I nodded. "That's okay. Don't feel guilty. This is hard. We have plenty of people."

The medical investigator arrived wearing sweatpants and a jacket. Sound asleep, now this. She took pictures and asked us to remove the sheets. We did.

She finished and then nodded at us to begin the extrication.

We went to work, cutting, prying, and slowly pulling the car apart.

There was no rush.

First, we methodically took the front passenger door off. We passed the door to one another and tossed it into the weeds. Many old hands gently, softly, held the girl in the front seat, eased her out, and carried her carefully down onto the roadway.

Three teenagers were sitting in the back seat. They were white, peaceful, leaning on one another. We repeated our sequence, cutting the door, gently lifting them out one by one.

Four white bags were lined up on the roadbed. We lifted each child and laid them in a bag. We zipped the bags up, one by one. That was the hardest moment because it had such finality.

The medical investigator's van arrived to transport the kids to the morgue. I went up to the young driver and told him that there were four DOAs.

He was irritated and complained, "No one told me there were four."

His attitude astonished me, but I just turned and walked

away, even as I heard him mutter to himself, "Maybe I can stack the bodies..."

Then we were done.

But none of us wanted to go home and be alone. The radio came alive.

"Hondo, state police are requesting firefighters at Station Two to assist with kids and parents."

Tom asked three of us to head down to the fire station. I did, but I sat in my car for a few minutes and took a deep breath before walking into the big classroom with its fluorescent lights.

The kids were piled on one side of the room holding one another. They were sitting in chairs, sitting on laps, talking, crying into cell phones. They were separate from the parents and as far away as they could be from the room where the police were taking statements and where, one by one, couple by couple, the parents came and were told.

I stood and watched. I didn't know who was who, whether adults were parents of one of the fatalities or parents of the living. It was a room awash in pain. It became too much. Another firefighter nodded toward the bays where the trucks were parked. I whispered to the fire department chaplain that we'd be there if anyone needed help.

The group of firefighters stood in the big station bay where we could be alone. It was the twilight time after a tragedy when we live the illusion that it was a dream or a maniacal practical joke, as if the four kids would at any minute walk into the station and laugh at how naive we were to believe that they were dead!

We were just playing dead! Then everyone would laugh together.

It startled us when the tones for our department rang out, and the dispatcher's tired voice announced, "Hondo, motor vehicle crash, rollover, possible alcohol involved. I-25, mile marker 288 northbound. Time out, 05:34."

Someone whispered under his breath, "You have to be fucking kidding."

It was still a dark night, black as crows. The new crash was less than a mile from the location of the first crash. We rolled an engine and ambulance.

We arrived on the new scene to find an SUV on its roof. The driver was on the ground, half out of the driver's door. Two sheriff's officers were already on scene and angry.

The guy had clearly been drinking, but he didn't seem badly hurt. We put him on a spineboard. We placed a C-collar on his neck and carried him to the ambulance. No one spoke or tried to cheer him up and say, "The worst is over."

It was 6:30 AM before we cleaned up after this crash. I was released and went home. I took a shower. I got in bed.

I was afraid to fall asleep, but I was exhausted. Finally, I drifted off, and the nightmares bloomed. Vivid details appeared: a used airway on the roadbed. Sheets over the car. A medic waving at me to help. Someone crying. The smell of digested alcohol.

I heard a phone ring. I opened my eyes. It rang again. I looked in the bed next to me. Laurie was already up and gone. I picked up my cell phone and looked at the time. It was a little after eight.

A girl's voice. She was wildly crying. I could only barely understand. "Hersch, what happened? Are they dead? Please say no, please..."

I recognized the voice as one of my daughter's best friends.

That's when it flooded back; the scene, the faces, and all those small-town kids. They were kids I knew. I didn't recognize them at the time. We were so focused on our work that I never looked to see who they were. But now I could see their faces. These were kids from my daughter's school and kids from town that everyone knew.

I was shocked.

All I could get out was "I'm sorry."

She wailed.

I said, "I'll call you as soon as I know more."

During the days after the crash, there was no escape. It was in the papers, on CNN. We had to drive by the crash scene to get to work, to the station, to get to town. For days after, people were always there. There were flowers, drawings, and pictures laid on the roadbed. I worried and obsessed that someone — another drunk — might plow into all the people standing on the shoulder. Driving by the scene a few days after, I recognized one of the dads. I pulled over and stopped. I got out, walked over; he hugged me, and I left.

The day after the crash, hanging out at the station, we talked about the call. Mike spoke and summed up how we all felt. He said, "I just want the parents to know that we treated them as if they were asleep and we didn't want to wake them."

CHAPTER TWENTY

THE NEXT FEW MONTHS
ARE GONNA SUCK

I can accept the idea of my own demise, but I am
unable to accept the death of anyone else.

— MAYA ANGELOU, "When I Think of Death"

Sixteen firefighters and EMTs were sitting in a circle in
a barren room at our fire station. We were in a critical
incident stress debriefing session a few days after the call
with the teens. These are rare, but we do them after calls we
know have emotionally affected one or more members of the
department.

Arms were crossed, folks were looking at their feet. It was
quiet. The facilitator patiently waited.

Finally, a burly paramedic looked at us all and said what
we were thinking: "The next few months are gonna suck."

Most nodded in assent.

There is a bit to unpack here. First, most of us had traveled this road before, and we knew difficult times were ahead.
But we also knew, because we'd been through this before, that
it wasn't a permanent condition. Winter would visit our souls
for a while, but eventually, spring would come. Most people

who don't experience tragedy regularly don't have that perspective. The first time tragedy comes, the future looks grim, full of pain. It feels as if our life has changed dramatically and irrevocably forever.

Yet what we learn, and what we need to cling to, is that we are designed to heal, not only physically but emotionally.

The paramedic was acknowledging two critical things: We can't avoid pain, stress, and grief, but these are only temporary. Can trauma and loss result in long-lasting effects? Yes. Approximately 20 percent of firefighters and other first responders suffer from post-traumatic stress disorder that can last for years. PTSD is a serious psychiatric disorder caused by exposure to trauma.

But the initial stress and grieving process is usually temporary. This doesn't lessen or minimize the pain of this period, but it helps to realize the sun will come up again. It is important to remember, even if it is written on a small note on the fridge, that this too shall pass.

In the immediate aftermath of a bad call, my process starts with dreams. After the call with the kids, I dreamed of the scene. I had flashbacks in my sleep: bunker gear on the roadway, the demolished cars, vivid colors and smells. Those dreams usually last a few weeks, although even years later I can still have them.

At the same time, during those first few weeks, I don't "feel" anything, not sadness nor remorse. I used to feel guilty that I didn't feel anything, but now I realize that it is just part of how I deal with trauma and loss.

Then, predictably, I get angry; irrationally borderline-crazy angry.

A few weeks after this call, I was with my brother at

lunch, and he mentioned that he had just hired a kid to do computer work who was a recovering heroin addict.

Something in me snapped.

"Screw him!" I yelled. "Goddamn addicts, there is no such thing as a recovering addict. Fuck 'em."

My brother looked at me like I had lost my mind — I had! I sat there and wondered: *I don't even believe what I just said. Where did that come from?*

The following week I was standing in line at the concession stand at a high school basketball game with a friend. She mentioned that the New Mexico state legislature had again voted against mandatory jail time for first-time DWI offenders. During the session, a state legislator had been quoted as saying, "I'm sick of hearing about punishment, punishment, punishment. These people need treatment!"

My friend said, if minors were arrested for DWI, legislators didn't want to put seventeen-year-old girls and boys in jails with adults.

Again without any warning, I blew up. I said, "I don't care how old they are, put them in jail. They're criminals."

She looked at me, shocked. But I didn't care. I thought: *Others can be compassionate. I want every drunk driver locked up.*

After weeks of silence, I became obsessive about wanting to talk about the call in detail. Intense calls — intense experiences — can have a fragmented quality. There is a need to make sense of it, to put the narrative together, to connect all the parts. This is "normal" for me — a milepost on my grief road — but hard on others. I have discovered these conversations are best held only with other firefighters who were there.

A month or so after the call, on a late night when we had just returned from some uneventful call, I stood with another firefighter outside the bay of our station under the night sky, and we talked about the fact that, on the night of that call, neither one of us could believe the kids were dead. They looked so peaceful sitting there. These conversations are an important part of healing, but they are best with people who shared the original experience. Together, we both shared our feelings, our deeply irrational beliefs, as we both wrote a story for ourselves that made sense.

At some point, after three to six months or so, the emotional charge lessened, and I've learned — like Dan — to put bad calls in a box in my mind, lock them up, and toss the key. This is a way to say to myself, *It's over now, time to get back to life.*

That is my familiar grief road, traveled many times now. It is a messy process, it is not linear, but the steps are predictable.

And of course, we never truly forget. As Dan experienced, that box gets opened from time to time. Something cues a memory — an anniversary, birthday, dream, or event — and we relive the pain. Or we remember the past without the pain and maybe feel guilty that the pain is gone.

It's important to realize that everyone's process — everyone's sense of tragedy, loss, and grief — will be different. Some feel as if they are going crazy, or they feel absolutely lost. Some find handrails — like faith, community, a spouse — that keep them grounded. There is no one way.

Yet one aspect of grieving seems universal: We often feel alone. When we grieve, we need to seek community, to find a place where we can share and speak and be heard. Firefighters have a built-in community; it is what saves us and keeps us sane. On calls, we often encounter the cauldrons of other people's pain and suffering, yet afterward, firefighters take care of one another. We check in. We call. We drag people to lunch. We let them talk. We have a couple of beers. We let old guys tell dark jokes. We allow young firefighters to cry, "What the fuck?" We let them know the next few months are gonna suck, but we'll get through them together.

Clearly, it is inescapable that if we love, if we care, we will eventually lose what we love and we will suffer that loss. This is part of the whole, part of being human. We love, we grieve, and we survive.

CHAPTER TWENTY-ONE

WHEN THE CARING COMES BACK

Doing without the best intentions leads to doing with the best intentions.

— THE TALMUD

There are times as you swim out of the deep and upward toward the surface that you feel numb, that you feel nothing, your compassion is gone, your ability to share any emotion has withered.

For example, a few months after the crash with the teenagers, I was helping a woman who had attempted suicide walk to our ambulance. Her distraught daughter was with us, and halfway down the walk, indifferent to her emotional state, I turned and asked her, "Didn't you go to day camp with my daughter?" The daughter looked at me like I was crazy, which at the time I guess I was.

On another call, helping a terrified woman who had just had a stroke, I remember thinking, *Cool! Classic stroke symptoms.*

This is called compassion fatigue — when your "emotional intelligence quota" drops to zero.

Another time, five of us — I and another firefighter, my sister (who is a firefighter-paramedic in a neighboring district), and my brother and his wife — were sitting having coffee. We were talking about a fatal bicycle crash that had just happened involving an acquaintance of my brother, also an avid cyclist.

The other firefighter and I immediately began discussing, to the horror of my brother and his wife, the mechanics of a cyclist versus train collision and whether or not it might have been suicide.

My sister, seeing that we weren't noticing the emotions of my brother and his wife, pointed at us, said, "Compassion fatigue," and told us to shut up.

Too many bad calls with rotten outcomes can push people into the deep end of the pool.

After tragedy, it first feels like you're wrenched through every emotion possible, from sadness to anger to terror and more. When it becomes exhausting, too much, you default to numbness, and this includes numbness to the emotions of others. It is like you don't understand why other people are sad, why they are angry, frustrated, or happy. You just don't get it.

When I reached this point after the crash, I started taking cues from those around me. Even though I felt nothing, when others showed empathy, I did the same.

By pretending, I became an expert at faking it. I mentioned this to a friend, Mitch Litrofsky, whose surprising rabbinic wisdom has been a lifeline for me more than a few times.

Over beers, I confessed to Mitch, "I just seem to be going through the motions now. I don't seem to care about the patients we see. I don't seem to be able to care."

Mitch smiled and replied, "Going through the motions is important. In the Talmud, the thought is expressed this way, 'Doing without the best intentions leads to doing with the best intentions.' You keep doing the work, and eventually, the caring will come back."

My dad often said the same thing in a different way, "Fake it until you make it."

I took their advice. For months after the crash, for almost a year, I kept faking it. Then the following spring, we were paged to a cardiac arrest.

I arrived a little after our ambulance. The patient was in his fifties, with untreated diabetes, high blood pressure, and a history of strokes. His wife watched in horror, hands over her mouth, as we hauled him off the couch, ripped off his shirt, started compressions, placed the defibrillator pads on his chest, and started an IV on his arm. She made the sign of the cross as we gave him drugs, then defibbed once, then twice, then a third time. When the lead paramedic finally shook his head, she collapsed to her knees, sobbing.

I was closest to her. I automatically knelt by her and put my hand on her arm. She put her head on my shoulder and cried. I didn't say anything. There is nothing that you can really say. It's sometimes best to just be quiet. Yet right there, at that moment, I felt bad for her. I felt sad again.

What I've learned through all of this is, first, naming things is essential. Now, after a bad call, when I slowly slip into not feeling anything, I can say to myself, "I have compassion fatigue again." It's exactly like saying, "I have the flu." I know I will suffer the symptoms for a while, but I've had it before, and I know it will pass. I know it is not a character flaw in me, and it is not permanent.

Next, I've learned to tell the individuals I'm close to, family and friends, when I am experiencing it. Again, to me, it is like telling someone you have the flu. This is helpful for two reasons. First, it helps others understand that you're not an unfeeling jerk. Second, it helps break down the stigmas over mental illness, even the temporary kind.

Finally, I've learned that it's okay at times to fake it till you make it. It goes against the grain to say — ever — don't be your authentic self. But sometimes, especially after a tragic event, you literally are not in touch with who you are. You are floating in space. When that happens, fake it until the shock wears off, until you feel again, until your compass quits spinning, and you can stand on your own.

CHAPTER TWENTY-TWO

I WILL NEVER BE THE SAME, BUT I WILL GET BETTER

> The death of a beloved is an amputation.
>
> — C.S. LEWIS, *A Grief Observed*

I have hewn carefully to my experiences with the fire department to explore the process of loss and grieving. Yet it begs the question: When the loss is personal, do the same rules apply? When it is someone close to you, is it the same road?

I would say yes. The road is the same, but it cuts deeper and goes through a much darker wood.

When my sister Susie died of cancer — three weeks after the physician's assistant wrote "leptomeningeal carcinomatosis" on the whiteboard — the world crashed down on us. Even though we knew it was coming, I was shocked when it happened. I became numb, then angry, I had dreams, I lost my sense of compassion, and I lost any sense of who I was or what I was supposed to do. Coping with this tragedy, I went down the same road as I do as a firefighter, except the pain was more intense, and a new feeling, worry for my nieces and nephew, bloomed fully.

I was great at faking it, at compartmentalizing grief, until I wasn't. On a walk around our house two weeks after Susie died, I collapsed on the path and just sobbed. A deeper cut, a darker wood.

But you know what we do after we collapse? We get up. Not because we want to, but because there is nothing else to do. It may take minutes or days, but we get up and move. On the fire department after bad calls, we all show up at the department and clean tools, put back equipment, and fuel the trucks. It is what we do because it has to be done and there is nothing else that can be done.

Time Shows Up

A trauma therapist once mentioned to me that, after trauma, time shows up. What she meant was that all the things on our calendar, all the events that keep us busy, shrink in importance, and we are left with time on our hands. Even though we are in motion and the clock ticks away, part of us is outside ourselves, still, and outside of time. Life moves on but we stop.

Trauma bends time in other ways. Afternoons seem to creep by. The formalities of death — funerals, obituaries, eulogies, gatherings, comforting — are mileposts. They are events we dread but have to get through. We wear dark suits and dresses, sit with our legs crossed in pews, on benches. We listen to soft voices. Listen to singing slightly off pitch. We hold back tears, maybe we laugh as we tell stories. The days move slowly, as if to ensure that we fully embrace the moments, that we are not in denial that someone has passed.

Then comes the time when all the functions are done, and we are alone. Those are the hardest times, when the ceremonies are over, and the full weight of a death presses down.

And we know at that exact moment, that tick on the clock, that we will not "recover."

I have a problem with the word *recover*. It implies that after trauma we somehow recover to a former state. Closer to the truth is that we get better, but we don't go back to the way things were, the way we felt, the innocence we had. We get better, but we are permanently altered. We incorporate those events into ourselves, and they change us.

It is akin to when we break a bone or have major surgery. We heal, but we know that something is different. We can feel it.

But life does take over. After the death of Susie, I discovered the inexorability of living and healing. It is a force; it is not passive. It is akin to a river in flood. We try mightily to hold on to trees, to branches, to hold on to the grief and pain because we feel like we should. But the river is powerful, and eventually, it catches us and sweeps us in its current toward the future.

We will have memories, flashbacks, aching moments of sadness. We are changed, but our lives, who we are and will be, belong to the future.

Field Notes: On Grieving

Here is my advice for this time when we are swept away by grief. These are thoughtful and practical ideas from the fire department, which are labeled "what to do after trauma":

1. Keep day-to-day life simple for a while.
2. You will feel as if you can't think, or all you can think about will be how you feel. This is normal. It will pass.
3. You may want to obsessively talk about the loss, or you may want everyone else to quit talking about it. Both normal.
4. Don't make any significant changes. Don't leave your job, spend a lot of money, sell your house, move, get a divorce, get a pet, have an affair, or start drinking.
5. Be prepared to wander aimlessly, to be easily distracted, to be lost for a while.
6. Accept your vulnerability. Seeing trauma and death makes us understand how vulnerable we are.
7. You may have emotional outbursts. You may get drunk once. These are normal responses to dealing with an abnormal situation.
8. Don't feel guilty when the pain of losing someone starts to lessen. This is a natural part of the healing process. Letting go is one of the hardest things we have to do.

Letting Go

The Southwest has a tradition of *descansos*, the crosses along roadways that mark where someone died in a crash. *Descanso* roughly translates to "resting place." I've always hoped it was a place where people's spirits, or their last seconds of consciousness, had a moment of peace between the violence and terror of a crash and then their leaving us.

The myth of the *descansos* is that the ghosts remain but not for everyone to see. The firefighters and police who were there see them. We see them sitting there in our imaginations.

A few weeks after the crash with the teenagers, three crosses and a Star of David appeared at the site, just off the roadway.

Afterward, I drove by it every day on the way to the station or to work.

Driving by *descansos* is a lesson in letting go. For the first six months, each time I drove by this one, I would remember the scene in detail, and I would think through all the things we did and could've done better.

But eventually my experience changed. I would see it and think, *We did the best we could. We saved the driver.*

Of course, I don't need *descansos* to be reminded of that scene or of the myriad others that have happened over thirty years. Now, when I'm reminded of tragedy and grief, I've learned to say to myself, *Huh, I had another nightmare*, or *I'm thinking about that crash again*. I watch those thoughts and dreams come and go. I don't try to block them or medicate them away. They are just part of who I am.

This is the experience of letting go, which is partially existential, realizing that tragedy, trauma, and death are all part of living. Whether we want them to be in our lives or not, they are ever present. It is also how we survive emotionally. The ability to let go, even when we want to cling to those branches in a flood, is how we resume our lives after tragedy.

Letting go takes a conscious effort and maybe a ceremony or two. It takes saying, "It's time to move on now," and then letting the river take you. Letting go does not mean we will forget, that the individuals we lost will no longer be in our memories. But we belong with the living, and so we need to let go of the dead. This is easy to write and often hard to do, yet it is part of this grand and glorious adventure.

Let go, live your life. It is okay.

Field Notes: Susie's Walk

I discovered a simple recipe for grief. It is not a cure; only time is the cure.

Because I didn't know what else to do after my sister died, what I did was walk.

It sounds simplistic but hear me out.

I'd leave the house early in the morning, in the twilight, when I was barely awake, early enough so that I wouldn't run into anyone and have to be polite and talk.

And I took my dogs. The dogs were eager to go, and their enthusiasm pulled me out of the house and the desire to do nothing. The dogs were so present, noses down, smelling the morning, listening to the coyotes. With dawn breaking, they taught me to be present, in the moment, with grief. It opened me up. For forty minutes, I was enveloped in the feelings of loss, of pain.

It became my ceremony. Each morning started with that walk for my sister.

After a few months, the pain softened. After a year, I could hold other thoughts on the walk.

Today, I still walk. I get up and out first thing in the morning. I will never "recover" — my grief is diminished, not gone — but I've let go.

part five

BE BRAVE.
BE KIND.
FIGHT FIRES.

The purpose of life is not to be happy. It is to be useful, to be honorable, to be compassionate, to have it make some difference that you have lived and lived well!

— LEO ROSTEN

At the start of this book, I noted that firefighters learn to thrive — living robustly, fully, and with joy — *because* of the calamity and heartbreak we see. Not, as one might think, *despite* what we experience.

Why is this so?

First, of course, is the simple fact that when you are familiar with death and suffering, you become profoundly and daily grateful to be alive and well. We also experience working together in a cause greater than ourselves, and we know we make a difference, however small, in the lives of people, in our community.

Being a firefighter teaches this substrate of thriving, the core elements of living a remarkable, joyful life. They are not unfamiliar or new. However, we practice them regularly, and practice is how anyone finds and realizes what we all hope for: a life of meaning and joy.

Here I want to make a distinction between happiness and joy. I feel happy when I get my car fixed and it actually runs. Or when I watch the US women's soccer team win the World Cup. Happiness arises when things turn out well.

Joy comes from within, from our actions, intentions, and

caring. Joy is being with people we love. The satisfaction of doing good work. Knowing our actions make a difference.

The distinction seems fine, but joy is what we are after. A joyful life is the goal.

In part 5, I focus on "praxis," which refers to practice or practical application. It means taking the steps to put an idea into action. Each chapter introduces one practice that can help you on the road to creating a meaningful and joyful life.

CHAPTER TWENTY-THREE

BE BRAVE

Life is always on the edge of death, always, and one
should lack fear and have the courage of life.

— JOSEPH CAMPBELL, *The Power of Myth*

Shanksville, Pennsylvania, is 1,694 miles from Santa Fe. It
was the Shanksville Volunteer Fire Department — forty
members, sixty or so calls a year — that first responded to
the crash of United Airlines Flight 93 on 9/11. They found
only fire, smoke, pieces of the airplane, and incinerated body
parts.

The World Trade Center in Manhattan is 1,984 miles
from Santa Fe. In total, 343 NYFD firefighters climbed the
stairs to the towers to rescue people; all were killed when the
towers collapsed.

In our department, Hondo, we have firefighters with
asthma and arthritis. We have firefighters struggling with
anxiety and claustrophobia. A few have anger issues. One
has PTSD from Iraq. Some struggle financially and have
troubled relationships. We have old guys — even older than
me — with stiff hands who struggle to get into gear at night.

The 343 NYFD firefighters were mostly in their thirties and forties. Some were in their twenties, and others were in their fifties and even sixties, my age.

Yet none of them were Odysseus or Achilles. All of them, each one, were like us: fallible human beings, joined by common cause. All of them suffered the same afflictions that are part and parcel of the human condition.

That morning, life asked them that most terrifying question, *Are you brave?* These 343 individuals, people just like you and me, people trained to be brave and useful, said yes.

After 9/11, a younger firefighter asked me, "Is courage something you learn, or is it something you're born with?"

Without thinking, I said you learn it. Maybe my answer was a way to address the doubts inside me, the question I had. Had I learned enough, did I have the courage, to do what the 343 did? Courage isn't the absence of fear. Courage is the ability to climb those steps while you are scared, while you are praying that you won't die. That's heroism.

Most firefighters don't think of themselves as heroic. Although many begin the career enamored with the idea of being a hero, most don't want to die on the job. And you can't plan heroic moments.

Instead, all of a sudden, out of the blue, life asks if you're ready, and you have to make a choice. On the fire department, there may be a familiar hand on the shoulder. Or, on impulse, you may put your hand on the shoulder of the firefighter next to you. The message: There is work to be done. There are people who depend on us.

So you take one step forward.

Firefighters absorb this in their pores, surrounded by a culture, by brothers and sisters, who share common cause, who share history that reaches back into the distant past. In that moment, we may be terrified, but we think, *I could not live with myself if I let my brothers and sisters down. I could not live with myself if I didn't do everything in my power to save someone.* That's the creed. But you don't know if it's taken root inside until the moment life asks.

Always, it is not up to us what life asks. It's up to us to choose how we will respond.

Everyday Brave

Of course, we are not asked every day to "risk a lot to save a lot" — my definition of heroism. But life regularly presents us with everyday opportunities to be brave.

Take a moment to unearth the choices you've made on any given day. Are there not decisions made, actions taken or not taken, based solely on whether you were brave in that moment? What we do often comes down to whether or not we have the fortitude to choose a more difficult path rather than avoid it.

Typically, we rationalize and cover up our less-than-courageous choices. I can think of hundreds of choices I have made out of anxiety or fear simply because I never asked the question, What is the bravest thing I can do? From skipping hard classes in college to walking away from seemingly challenging job opportunities to not asking someone out, multiple times I have avoided the bravest path.

Yes. Unquestionably choosing the bravest path means a life with some failures, rejection, losses, and times of discomfort. But as Nietzsche reminded us, what doesn't kill us only makes us stronger.

In other words, by seizing those daily opportunities, not only do we live a fuller life, but we prepare ourselves for the biggest challenges that living presents.

I think of everyday brave in two ways. First, it's the willingness to live without illusions. The world is a dark yet wondrous place, and to live here fully is not for the weak-hearted. For example, to love someone means inviting grief, through either loss of love or death, since we all die eventually. But not to love cuts us off from the primal experience of being human.

Second, everyday brave means pushing away comfort. Kahlil Gibran wrote that comfort is something that comes into our house as a guest, and it soon becomes the host and then the master. The quest for comfort shrinks our lives. We make choices to avoid what is uncomfortable. But discomfort defines the brave path, and it is the only path to growth. Let me repeat: Doing uncomfortable things, stuff that is a little scary, is the only path to becoming who we are meant to be.

Training for a Brave Life

At least if the species has lost its animal strength,
its individuals can have the fun of finding it again.

— TERRY AND RENNY RUSSELL, *On the Loose*

My first piece of practical advice is not to wait for life to ask, *Are you brave?* Instead, whenever you face a decision, big or small, intentionally ask yourself, "What is the bravest choice?"

At a personal level, this question often cuts to the chase. If we are honest with ourselves, it can help illuminate why we make the decisions we do, and it often points us toward the path that may be more difficult but is, in the long run, more fulfilling.

Most of the time, most of us — when facing a tough choice — ask ourselves the question, "What is the most short-term, comfortable thing to do?" Often, that question doesn't even rise to the level of consciousness; we automatically react in whatever way that leads down the path of comfort.

For example, before I became a firefighter and EMT, I was put off (to put it mildly) by blood, gore, and anything medical. The idea of doing CPR on someone made me light-headed. I would immediately change the subject if a conversation drifted off into topics medical. I thought I was just born that way. Avoidance was my strategy.

After I became a firefighter, I realized I would have to do something about my "see blood and run" reaction.

As I learned, if you want to tackle something big, start small. I didn't try to "get over" my medical anxieties and issues by going on serious trauma calls. Instead, I signed up for an evening first-aid class, which taught us how to treat bumps and bruises, sprains, and simple fractures. I survived. That under my belt, I took a CPR class, and it was okay! I got through it. Finally, a year later, I signed up for more discomfort: a six-month EMT class. We did rotations in the emergency room and got to do a lot of hands-on EMT stuff. I struggled, but by then, I was as intrigued as I was put off by some of the cases. I started going on medical and trauma calls with the fire department — small stuff at first, and always with experienced medics. Eventually, dealing with medical trauma became second nature for me. About three years after my first-aid class, I became comfortable in that world.

Did that make me brave in all aspects of my life? To keep things in perspective, later on when my daughters were teenagers, I was always nervous to tell them to clean their rooms. Bravery in one area doesn't necessarily translate to others.

That said, I learned a crucial lesson: The most daunting obstacles become manageable when you break them down into smaller chunks. When following the brave path, take small steps, and overcome fear in stages.

The goal is to live as fearless a life as possible, but that doesn't mean never feeling fear. It means, from wherever you stand right now, moving forward and asking the question — as often as possible: What is the bravest choice?

In *Gulliver's Travels*, by the eighteenth-century satirist Jonathan Swift, the "giant" Gulliver is tied down with a hundred tiny ropes by the Lilliputians. In the same way, we are often "tied down" by hundreds of anxieties and fears that keep us from becoming who we are meant to be, fearless. Asking, "What is the bravest choice?" and doing the work of attacking our fears, rather than accepting them, is how we break those threads.

We may never be asked to save someone's life while risking our own. We may never have to enter a burning building or jump onto subway tracks to pull someone out of the way of an oncoming train.

Yet every day, life is asking us, *Are you brave?* Every day.

Field Notes: Be Brave

1. Identify three people you would describe as brave. Explain why. The stories of others can be powerful examples for us.
2. Identify three situations in the past where you made brave choices, where you asked, "What is the bravest

path I could take?" Write down those stories. If you dig in, you will find plenty of stories of you making brave choices.

3. Identify three examples where you chose to make the comfortable choice instead of the brave choice. Think about what you could have done differently. Most often, we choose comfort because we are afraid of rejection, failure, losing, or being emotional uncomfortable (for example, being embarrassed). None of those will kill us, but we often act as if they will.

4. Name the fear. It helps to name what we are afraid of — such as, "In this situation, I was afraid of being rejected" — instead of allowing fear to grow as an unnamed anxiety in our imaginations.

5. Pick one current situation where making a brave choice would make a difference. Start simple, keep it small to begin with. As you get more experience, you can go for the bigger fish.

6. If you get stuck, ask these questions:

   - What is the best that could happen?
   - What is the worst that could happen?
   - What will happen if I do nothing?

7. Remind yourself that, in the pursuit of a brave life (as opposed to a life seeking comfort), failure, rejection, and discomfort are part of the terrain. But they will not kill you or demean you! They are badges of honor in pursuit of a meaningful life. To get what we want out of our only life, we need to take risks.

CHAPTER TWENTY-FOUR

BE KIND

If you want others to be happy, practice compassion. If you want to be happy, practice compassion.

— DALAI LAMA, *The Healing Power of Meditation*

The most difficult act of bravery is often kindness.

A veteran career firefighter and I were walking out of the gym. As we turned to go to our cars, we noticed a man on the ground, apparently drunk, lying against the curb in the parking lot. It was one of those city locations where drunks and the homeless congregate. He had tangled, long dark hair and a beard with a touch of gray. He was dressed in old jeans, tennis shoes, and a jacket, with a thin blanket around his shoulders.

Typically, people deal with this kind of situation in one of three ways. The most common is disregard: We don't see the person; they are invisible. The second is scorn: We assume they are addicts and drunks; less than us. The third is kindness. My friend went over, knelt down, and woke the man up. "Dude," he said in a nonjudgmental, gentle voice. "You're going to get hurt if you sleep here." He helped the man to his feet, and the man continued on his way.

In his career, my friend had encountered hundreds of drunks. I would not have been surprised if he had just rolled his eyes, his compassion withered. But he didn't; he was kind and compassionate.

Therein lies the practice: small acts of kindness.

There are a hundred reasons not to help a stranger passed out in a parking lot. It's potentially dangerous. The person might be "crazy," have a communicable disease, or smell. The situation isn't our problem, we're busy and don't have time, and so on.

Despite all that, my friend offered a helping hand and gentle words.

Becoming a firefighter opens your eyes to suffering. And it is not "drive-by" awareness. We are immediately engaged in the human drama; the blood, the tears, the goop, the smells, and the pain that emanates on the street.

It is transformative.

We learn that everyone has suffered, everyone has a story. Some of those stories, well, you wonder how an individual can still be standing. There was the elderly woman who lived alone, all her belongings packed up and labeled, ready to die, but with no one to talk to except us. The stressed-out professional couple, caring for a father with Alzheimer's who bolted one night; when we found him walking down the road, he told us he was going home to Cleveland.

Everyone has a story.

The understanding that everyone suffers changes your perception. You see individuals as more complex, sometimes as wounded, often as struggling with their own demons. But being moved by people's stories doesn't necessarily translate into doing something. Empathy doesn't always translate into compassion, into action.

Being a firefighter, our job is not just to understand, but to help. Our profession is defined by kindness in action, which is transformative.

How? Start by asking the question, What do firefighters get out of it? In the bigger picture, what do any of us get out of being kind? It's a fair question. Altruism sounds nice, a high and lofty goal, but day to day, in the midst of our busy lives, why be kind? Why make eye contact with the guy begging on the corner? Why risk life and limb to save someone from a fire?

Even ancient religions and philosophies struggle to answer this question, which boils down to: Why put someone else's interests above your own? I'm not interested in any rewards in an afterlife. What are the practical rewards right now, here, on this planet, in this lifetime?

Imagine this situation. You're stuck in traffic and late getting home. You're creeping along when all of a sudden the guy in the car behind you starts banging on his horn and flashing his headlights. You ignore this for a minute, but then you get upset. The honking and flashing continue, even though traffic has come to a complete stop. Other drivers are staring. Finally, you've had enough. Angry, you get out of your car to confront the jerk pounding his horn. Before you can say anything, the driver rolls down his window. He is in tears, sobbing. He cries, "My son was in an accident. They've taken him to the hospital. He's going into surgery! I need to get to him. If you just move aside, I can reach the off-ramp."

In an instant, you change. You tell him, "Follow me!"

Back in your car, you lead him onto the shoulder, onto the off-ramp, and bang your own horn as you race together to the hospital.

What happened?

This is the empathic shift. Without much thought, you put yourself in someone else's shoes; their son could be your child, hurt and alone in a hospital. Your worries about being late drop away and all you care about is helping this stranger.

Later, after the adrenaline rush is gone, you realize it feels good to help someone. It feels good to be needed and provide tangible help. It feels important to momentarily put aside your own concerns and be there for someone who is struggling or in danger. Ask any first responder, and they will describe a feeling of expanded presence; for a moment, they are involved in something larger than themselves.

This is the reward. This is the answer to the question. The *action* of compassion releases powerful feelings of connection, empathy, satisfaction, and joy.

The experience of people suffering is transformative. The action of helping is transformative squared.

Helping takes many forms. We write checks to charities; we sign petitions. But directly touching someone else, knowing you've made a specific difference in someone's life, is the most powerful. The great radical thinker, Jesus, didn't isolate himself in the temple and pontificate; he went among the people and washed the feet of lepers.

Doing. Helping. Taking action. These are the verbs that truly make a difference.

Daily, we have opportunities to be kind in all sorts of ways. Holding a door open, allowing another driver to turn first, comforting someone in pain, giving up our seat on a bus — all small acts of kindness that can ripple out and give us the feeling of making a difference.

Truthfully, on the fire department, most of what we do are small acts of kindness. On a call, firefighters commonly find small ways to help. They shovel a driveway for someone with chest pains, they help find scared animals after a fire, they put the furniture back. Nothing heroic. But it is what people remember. Except for ten-year-old kids, most people remember the little things, not the big red trucks with lights and sirens.

Kindness Killers

There are obstacles — kindness killers — that interfere with the impulse to be kind. Three of them are the most worrisome and common.

The first is righteousness. Once we responded to a rollover on a snowy January road. We got there to find the driver was drunk but unhurt, while his girlfriend was dead, having been ejected from the SUV. I remember cracking, losing my temper. I felt a wave of righteous anger that eliminated even the idea of feeling kindness or compassion for the driver.

Yet when I went home, I couldn't help but remember when I was eighteen. My girlfriend and I were driving home in a storm. We'd both had a beer. I lost control of the car, and we did a 360 on the interstate. We both held our breath, and then all of a sudden, we were fine, headed the right way with no traffic around us. We laughed.

Who was I to sit in judgment of this driver? The only difference between the two of us was I had better tires.

Righteousness, the belief that we are somehow morally

superior, can kill the impulse to be kind. This often plays out with how people treat addicts. If people believe that addiction is a "character flaw," they judge and condemn the individual. But if people realize addiction is a lifelong disease, they find it much easier to be kind when someone struggles.

Another kindness killer is self-involvement — the feeling that my problems are the most significant problems, that my life is the center of the universe. Of course, everyone gets wrapped up in their own world at times. Sometimes we forget that our problems, in the larger scheme of things, are often small and insignificant. Being a firefighter is a constantly humbling experience in this regard. When our pager tones out, we are usually thrown into situations where the problems are much larger than our own. It is a constant wake-up call, a reminder to keep things in perspective and to question our own sense of self-importance.

Finally, there is fear. When we are fearful of the suffering of others, we put on blinders so that we don't see suffering. Our concern is often what would happen if we let suffering in. We fear it might hurt us, that we aren't strong enough to shoulder it. Therefore, it is best to avoid it altogether.

My advice for coping with fear is twofold. First, accept that we can't avoid the suffering of others. It is something we all need to prepare for. Best to open yourself to it; best to explore the depth of your kindness.

Second, we are strong enough and our kindness is deep enough to deal with even the most difficult situations. For example, I know a woman who recently died of ALS. In her last year, her friends gathered around her, took turns feeding her and her family, and bathed her and took her out for walks. No one said, "I can't handle this." All rose to the occasion. There are hundreds if not thousands of stories occurring daily that demonstrate the ability to be kind under the hardest circumstances.

Radical Kindness

For every time life asks us, *Are you brave?*, life offers a hundred opportunities to be kind.

Indeed, personally, I think the road to "enlightenment" isn't only turning inward with meditation, but turning outward toward the world with "radical kindness." This is choosing daily to seek out opportunities to be kind, to make kindness your first impulse. Time spent being kind, searching out moments to be kind, will crack the universe open and teach us about ourselves and where we fit.

Radical kindness involves three principles: Do it daily, keep your ego out of it, and don't expect reciprocity.

1. Do It Daily

First, find daily moments to be kind, seek them out, plan for them to happen. Notice the door that needs to be opened, the woman in a rush whom you can let cut in front of you, or the child lost in the store. These moments are endless; we just need to see and seize them. These acts often take only seconds or minutes, and they require only a shift in our perspective.

2. Keep Your Ego Out of It

Have you ever held a door for someone who rushes by and says nothing? Did you feel slighted or put down, maybe a little invisible? That's your ego speaking.

Our egos are like balloons being inflated. Left unchecked, they will grow and take over our lives, until, you guessed it, something bursts them (which, trust me, will happen). An inflated ego gets upset if it's not immediately thanked and appreciated. "Wait," the ego says, "how can you not thank me for my brilliant act of kindness!? I opened a door for you!"

Our egos believe the world revolves around them. The ego is the self, weaponized: It defends, it attacks, it rationalizes, it lies. Its job is to protect you from any wounds, real or imagined.

When others cut in front of you on the interstate, beware of your ego: Is it really important for you to be one more car length ahead? Or is it more valuable and helpful — and egoless — to let the driver in?

3. Don't Expect Reciprocity

Let go of the idea of reciprocity. Altruistic reciprocity — I will do something good for you with the understanding that there will be payback — is built into human nature. The reward for radical kindness is in the act itself. The reward is that we've helped someone in need and that is enough.

We will not be perfect at this, and perfection is not the point. The point is learning the impact on ourselves and others of our acts of kindness. The point is expanding our sense of self, growing that sense that we are making a difference, however small, in this universe.

Field Notes: Acts of Kindness

1. The practice, if you are so inclined, is to pursue an act of kindness (or more) each day.

2. These acts don't have to be grand gestures; little actions work.

3. Recall the three principles of radical kindness:

   - **Do it daily:** Be intentional. Consciously look for opportunities to act in someone else's interest. Simple actions done for someone else can make a big difference.

   - **Keep your ego out of it:** Be forgiving. People are busy, people are self-involved. There is little we can do about that. But when we shift from "me-centered" to "other-centered" for a few moments, we can experience being "egoless." It is a powerful and positive feeling. Open the door and don't worry about being thanked.

   - **Don't expect reciprocity:** The goal is to be a positive force in the world, regardless of the consequences.

4. Make it a habit. We can find simple pleasure every day by being kind.

CHAPTER TWENTY-FIVE

BE USEFUL

Mankind was my business. The common welfare
was my business. Charity, mercy, forbearance, and
benevolence were all my business. The dealings of
my trade were but a drop of water in the comprehensive ocean of my business.

— MARLEY'S GHOST,
A Christmas Carol by Charles Dickens

Laurie wanted to talk about my truck. It was beaten up,
had a lot of miles on it, but it had helped me tow engines and ambulances out of the mud, deliver generators up
challenging driveways, and run on innumerable calls in the
middle of the night in all kinds of weather. I had a relationship with that vehicle.

Laurie thought otherwise.

"Your Suburban is a piece of crap....We should sell it."

I shook my head. I loved that truck. "But..."

Laurie raised her hand.

REEEE! My pager vibrated. "Hondo, structure fire, mutual aid for El Dorado. Flames showing."

"Gotta go!" I said.

A difficult conversation was avoided. A few minutes later, driving the Suburban in the general direction of the fire, I heard on my fire department radio, "Explosion. The garage is fully involved, twenty-foot flames and black smoke. House is evacuated."

I parked a block away, pulled my gear bag out of the back, kicked off my shoes, and bunkered up: pants, jacket, and helmet. I grabbed a fire ax and a medical bag. We moved quickly into the tight group around the El Dorado chief. There was urgency in the air.

Mike, my partner that day, asked the chief, "How can we help?"

The chief yelled over the roar of the garage fire: "The explosion was in the garage, it's gone! We have a crew knocking down that fire from the outside. Gas and electric are turned off. We're going to set up a fan and send a crew through the front door. You four are the entry team. Two in, two out." The chief nodded at a group of firefighters.

He looked at the two of us. "Can you grab the vent fan off Engine Two and set it up?"

We both nodded; it was time to be useful. We lifted the big fan out of the engine, set it up in front of the door, and got it started. It would clear smoke out of the house as the team of two entered.

Later, we cut trenches into the roof to make sure fire hadn't spread. We used our thermal imaging camera to peer through the smoke and the walls to make sure we hadn't missed anything. Later that day, "useful" meant salvage: hauling wet, burnt, and twisted junk out of the garage.

By the end, we were exhausted, dehydrated, and hungry.

But there were fist bumps all around. We'd lost the garage but saved the home.

I drove home after the fire and pulled into our garage. I turned off the engine, and the Suburban shuddered a few times before it stilled. It was an old truck.

Laurie stood there smiling. She laughed as I, stiff and sore, got out of the truck and limped toward the house. She was a firefighter, so she knew why I was smiling; she knew the feeling of being useful.

She hugged me and whispered in my ear, "I guess you and that truck have a few more years left in you."

How Can I Help?

The question "How can I help?" is my favorite meditation and prayer. It's answered by the most essential spiritual shift anyone can experience. At that moment, we stop thinking of ourselves. At that moment, we exist for someone else; to help them, save them, comfort them, reduce their suffering. In that moment, we become courageous beyond measure. We become the fiercest of angels battling suffering and chaos.

The joy of being a firefighter is solving problems that others can't solve. From fighting a house fire to doing CPR on a dog — to cleaning a stove — we get to be useful. That, in my simple calculus, creates meaning. In other words, whether I am turning on a hydrant with a wrench or putting a C-collar on a patient, I feel engaged and part of something larger than myself. If only temporarily, in those moments, I am not self-obsessed. I am useful.

Wrench. Hammer. Kitchen. Computer. Shovel. Stethoscope. Wouldn't it be odd if all the tools for finding meaning in life were this simple? If the real answer for the quest for meaning wasn't a spiritual journey but rather work that solved problems, work that was useful?

A small yet revolutionary premise: Our fulfillment in life is not linked to money, fame, or status — as alluring as they might be. It is directly connected to our ability to be useful, to do work in service to others.

In our culture, this premise can cause angst because it is counterintuitive. We swim in a sea of money, fame, and status. Media inundates us with the 24/7 message that life is about beauty and riches. Individuals spend their lives thinking: *If I only got into this college, had this job, this amount of money, that car, house, vacation — this number of followers on social media — then I would be fulfilled.*

But it is an illusion.

I once taught a class to final-semester high school seniors on meaning. One student presciently wrote this as part of an assignment: "My parents spent a lot of money for me to go to this prep school so that I could get into a good college so then I could get a well-paying job so then I could afford to send my kids to a prep school....What's the point?"

The illusion that we share — to greater or lesser degrees — is that money and status are our tickets to a fulfilling life.

The psychologist Mihaly Csikszentmihalyi studies what makes people happy, and he notes that, according to studies, the average number of people who say they are "very happy" — about 30 percent — hasn't changed over time, even though personal income — adjusted for inflation — has almost tripled over the last sixty years. Other studies have found that at a certain point — about $60,000 a year, give or take — more material wealth doesn't seem to correlate with increased happiness.

Then what is the path?

In any situation, ask, "How can I help?"

Or, Become a Volunteer Firefighter

Of course, to me, the preferred way to help others is to become a volunteer firefighter! No, that's not required for a fulfilling life, but exploring why individuals choose this work highlights the core elements of fulfillment.

Plus, I know a lot of firefighters, and over the years, I've asked them the same question: Why did they become a firefighter? Career firefighters are not motivated by the money, and for volunteers, of course, there is no money. Either way, the pressure is similar, the work is stressful, the hours are often terrible, and the lifestyle can be amazingly inconvenient. Just ask the spouse or significant other of a volunteer.

Firefighters have answered my question in many different ways, but their responses usually cluster around three basic intentions or needs.

1. To Help People

For some people, the desire to help is as natural as breathing. They see need in their world and their instinct is to go toward it, to help solve the problem. Obviously, this is not unique to firefighters. It is innate in many. Once during a blizzard, an SUV with a family slid off the interstate into an arroyo at high speed. No one was seriously injured, but what made it stick in my mind was seeing how many people stopped, got out of their cars, and ran to help. Wanting to help is a potent aspiration, and it is the primary motivation for any type of volunteer or first responder.

2. To Be Part of Something Bigger than Myself

A firefighter I interviewed told me he didn't want to be just a random individual nobody knew. He wanted to be part of something bigger than himself, doing good in the world. Firefighting provides this; working with others, we pull together to complete our task and solve problems. This in and of itself is a powerful and even addictive force. This country likes to tout individualism, yet the truth is that most great things are accomplished by a collective, by groups, by teams working together. From creating the Constitution to raising barns, from building ships to putting humans on the moon: Great accomplishments require people coming together to focus on tasks more significant than themselves.

3. To Fill a Void

It is not uncommon to wake up in the middle of an otherwise well-run life with the sense that something is missing. Whenever it happens, we find ourselves grappling with the classic existential questions: *Who am I? What is my life about? What is my purpose? What should I do with the rest of my life?*

Interestingly, among firefighters, a lot of new volunteers — men and women — are in their forties, fifties, and sixties, and they come from successful lives and happy families. But, in their words, there just seems to be a void. Call it a midlife crisis, but more than one middle-aged volunteer I spoke to expressed a craving for meaning.

They found it by being useful and helping others; volunteer firefighting became a simple answer to those existential questions. Once, on a training evening, a new sixty-something firefighter got to run the engine for his first time. After a few minutes, he exulted, "This is the best job ever!"

He had found, to use Joseph Campbell's word, his "bliss." He had found his meaning, and he was having fun.

Taking Our Own Vital Signs

In the field, when we assess a patient, one of the necessary actions is to look at their vital signs: Are they alert? What is their pulse, blood pressure, skin color? This helps us surmise whether a patient is sick and needs to be transported immediately or if we can "stay and play" — get more history, do a more thorough assessment, and so on.

In the same way, we often need to do a set of "vital signs" on ourselves. We can ask ourselves those big "vital" questions: *What is my life about? Have I created meaning? How am I useful? What should I do with the rest of my life?*

Thinking deeply about those questions often brings us to three actions we can take.

First, we can choose a profession that is our "important work," that aligns with what feels meaningful for us. Whatever the vocation, we feel as if we are contributing to the larger good and using our unique skills.

Second, we can reframe our existing job. I once interviewed a woman who worked on an assembly line putting together pediatric IV kits. Repetitive work. But she said it had two qualities that made it useful and part of her purpose. First, it was supporting her family, and second, she saw her work as not just assembling IV kits, but being part of the chain of individuals saving the lives of kids. This created meaning for her.

Third: volunteer. Based on the time you have and your circumstances, looking for the right volunteer opportunity can shift your priorities. This might be working at an animal shelter, coaching a kids' sports team, or even becoming a volunteer firefighter.

In all three of these examples, the goal is to suffuse our lives with meaning, to live a life with purpose. If we take to heart the lessons of the lifeline exercise in chapter 1 (page 16) — that our lives are finite — we feel urgency. We don't have time to lose. It might be that our important work in life is taking care of our families. Or it might mean quitting our job and working for a nonprofit. Or it could be coaching that Little League baseball team.

What is vital to grasp is that we are each here to do important work. Yet we can't wait for the universe to tell us what that important work is; it is up to us to create it, build it, and make it manifest.

Henry David Thoreau wrote, "The mass of men lead lives of quiet desperation." We can make a different choice, follow a path that we cut out of the morass of expectations, status, and illusions. It is the harder path, but being a volunteer firefighter has taught me that it is the fulfilling path. It is no fun to get up at two in the morning in the winter to fight someone else's fire, but at the end of the night, we can tell ourselves we made a difference, we did something important. That is being useful.

Field Notes: Your Important Work

The world is crying out for your talents, your useful work. Your community is in dire need of what you can contribute.

With that as a core understanding, let's explore how to be useful using your talents, focusing on that important work.

First, it is vital to know where your talents lie. What are you good at? What comes naturally? What work (work = energy focused on a task) makes you happy? Where do you like to put your energy?

Second, what gives you meaning? Everyone is different, but we can develop meaning in our lives. Write a meaning statement, like "I work to support my family," or "I use my accounting skills to help start-ups succeed," or "I volunteer with Habit for Humanity to build homes for the homeless." The key idea is to *develop* meaning, to make it happen, rather than wait for it to magically occur. This takes work, but the payoff is clarity about what you are here to do.

A good meaning statement is short, a paragraph or less. With talent and meaning defined, the next step is to find where you can be of the most help. Where is there a need? Consider the three actions I mention in this chapter.

1. Find a job that matches your "meaning" and talents and serves a need.
2. Reframe your job so that you see your work as serving a need.
3. Volunteer. Useful, important, and meaningful volunteer work, even for only a few hours a week, can make a significant and positive difference in how you feel about yourself.

CHAPTER TWENTY-SIX

BELONG

I want to be with people who submerge
in the task, who go into the fields to harvest
and work in a row and pass the bags along,
who are not parlor generals and field deserters
but move in a common rhythm
when the food must come in or the fire be put out.

— MARGE PIERCY, "To Be of Use"

After the bad call I describe in chapter 6 (page 49) — when a car crashed into the Galisteo River, and we saved everyone in the family but the mother — I learned one of the most important lessons that being a firefighter can teach: You can't do it alone. Firefighting is a communal, collective effort. It is people moving in common rhythm that makes the fire department work.

Up until that call, I'd been somewhat of a loner. After that call, I needed the department more than the department needed me.

All the department veterans had experienced calls that stuck with them. Hondo members had responded to the New

Mexico State Prison riot in 1980, which had involved decapitations, burnt bodies, stabbings, and rapes with broom handles.

On another call, one firefighter had done CPR on a cardiac arrest patient. He didn't realize it was a friend until the call was over and the patient was pronounced dead.

Four firefighters had been at the station cleaning up after a fatal car crash involving a teenage girl when the girl's mom showed up — not knowing about the crash — and asked if they had seen her daughter.

For decades, the fire department had developed an informal protocol for dealing with tragedies, difficult times, and bad calls. First, you get taken to lunch by the chief. I got my call a few days after my experience with the mom. I wasn't sleeping well. When I did sleep, I was having nightmares. I was repeatedly dreaming about the mom's belly turning blue.

I'm sure Laurie made the call to Dan and told him I was a mess.

Dan and I met in a deli, and he started by saying, "You look horrible." Diplomacy was not his strong suit. "So, how's it going?"

I shrugged. "It sucks. I've never felt this way. I can't get over the idea that if I would have done something different…"

Dan put his hand up. "That's bullshit. You can't think that way. It happened. It's over. There's nothing you can do. People die. Some people, no matter what you do, are trying hard to die. If they're going to die, they're going to die. There is nothing we can do."

He stopped for a minute, looked at the menu. The waitress came over, and Dan ordered a breakfast burrito. I asked for a turkey and green chili sandwich on rye.

The waitress spun on her heels and headed toward the kitchen.

Dan continued, "Some patients are doing everything they can to die. First, they have a head injury, and then they bust open an aorta. Then they arrest. It's just their time. They are going to die — like the mom — and all we can really do is hold their hands. Our job is not to save those people. We aren't surgeons; we don't have their training, their tools, or a clean ER with lots of light. We are out there in the mud with just our hands."

Dan took a sip of coffee.

"Our job is to save the people who are not going to die and get them to the hospital."

I leaned forward on my elbows. "But if I figured out that she had a bleed in her belly, if we had gotten two IVs started right away…"

Dan shook his head. "'What if' is bullshit. Then she would have died twenty minutes later. There was nothing you could do. She was going to die as soon as the seat belt dissected her aorta."

We ate for a while. The waitress brought us more coffee.

"Are you guys firefighters?" she asked. "It sounds pretty intense, what you're talking about. I couldn't help listening."

Dan answered. "Just a bad day on the department."

"Well, hang in there," she said. "We really appreciate what you guys do."

I smiled half-heartedly. She turned and went to the next table.

"Look," he said. "You can't think about it. No more 'what if.' We don't have that luxury. We just do the best we can and go home every night."

Dan thought a moment and then continued, "Our job is to be ready for the next fucked-up call and the next. Other people have the luxury of thinking. Our job is to be ready, to go and to help. If thinking gets in the way, then you have to stop thinking. Stop thinking about her, the family, and the scene."

I stirred sugar and cream into my coffee. I took a bite of my turkey sandwich. The green chili was hot, and my eyes watered.

I must have looked skeptical.

He smiled and said, "Hey, it works for me. Otherwise, you know me, I can be obsessive. I'd be thinking about them all the time. Then I'd start drinking. And stop talking. And stop painting. If I don't sell paintings, we're out on the street. Life would grind to a halt. Patty would eventually shoot me, dig a hole in the backyard, and toss me in. If anyone asked where I was, she'd just shrug."

I smiled at that.

"So look. Don't do anything stupid. Just give yourself some time."

After being taken to lunch by the chief, the second department strategy is not to leave you alone. Firefighters kept calling me to go out for breakfast or just to check in, to ask me if I could come down to the station and help roll up and catalog spare hose. They'd talk about their worst moments to let me know I wasn't alone.

This is the "brother- and sisterhood" of the fire department. It's tribe and family coming to the aid of one of their own.

Find Your Tribe

Humans are tribal beings. Small hunter-gatherer groups were our primary social structure long before agriculture and cities, those massive hives of strangers. Staying together in a small tribe was how we originally survived and evolved. As small, naked primates, the "lone ranger" setting out on his or her own had little chance of surviving, and this need to belong to a group is ingrained.

Healthy fire departments replicate that tribal spirit and fill that longing to belong.

There are three primary attributes that define a tribe, and all exist in fire departments. First, the physical work of firefighting is hard and often complicated. We have to work together, closely in a "common rhythm," or we can't do the work, whether that's fighting fires or carrying a hallucinating two-hundred-pound patient out of an upstairs bedroom. Tribes have goals that are impossible to accomplish alone.

Next, firefighting and rescue work is often shocking and emotionally draining. This creates a shared emotional bond that also defines a tribe. As a firefighter, you learn quickly that it's hard to talk about and share what you've seen and what you've done with the "outside world." The only folks who truly understand are the brothers and sisters in the fire department who share what you've been through. For this reason, tribes often turn inward, speak a private tribal language, tell the tribe's stories, and laugh and weep at their shared history.

Finally, fire departments spend a lot of time together. Our little department might gather twenty to thirty times a month. In the middle of the night, everyone arrives at a fire half-asleep, dressed in whatever they could grab from their closet, pillow heads, wild hair.

During the day, guys in suits or in T-shirts and jeans jump out of their cars and put on bunker gear. Women in dresses step into the heavy pants and boots or shed the dress behind a car and gear up.

Firefighters share difficult experiences when all the "social masks" are stripped away by exhaustion and anxiety. It is no wonder firefighters often say, "This is my second family. These are my brothers and sisters."

All healthy tribes share these attributes, like good sports teams, performance groups, and spiritual missions. I once helped rebuild a church in rural New Mexico — I was assigned to clean bat and pigeon poop out of the attic — and it was the same experience.

Thus, I believe that belonging to a team, a group, a tribe is a crucial practice for thriving and leading a meaningful life. We need others to solve complex problems, to care for one another, and to help survive dark times: It is who we are.

We ignore this longing at our peril. We live in a time that fosters isolation more than community. Social media, work and career demands, dispersed families, how we care for the elderly — we are more splintered, not less, by what should be common tasks that bring tribes together.

For me, belonging to a close-knit group was something I didn't know I needed until I needed it. Then the light bulb went on. The fire department has ruined forever — for me — the myth of the "individual." I would rather be submerged in a common task with others than stand on a peak alone.

Field Notes: Joining a Fire Department

You can join or create all kinds of tribes. If, after reading this book, you feel inspired to join a volunteer fire department, here is what to expect. If you have the time and inclination, it's worth it!

1. Most volunteer fire departments require no previous experience. You must be a minimum age and pass a basic physical agility test, and some require a psychological test.
2. Training is usually paid for by the department. Basic training typically involves fighting fires, hazardous materials awareness, emergency medical training, and wildland firefighting (depending on your location). Many departments also need people for administrative work.
3. Most departments train once or twice a week.
4. Some departments run as few as a hundred calls a year, others are in the thousands.
5. If you are an "on-call" volunteer, you carry a pager 24/7 and respond to calls as needed. A paid on-call firefighter gets paid a stipend per call. Or, there is shift work, and shifts can be eight to twenty-four hours.
6. To find the opportunities in your area, visit www .makemeafirefighter.org.

CHAPTER TWENTY-SEVEN

BE TOUGH

In these plethoric times when there is too much coarse stuff for everybody, and the struggle for life takes the form of competitive advertisement and the effort to fill your neighbor's eye, there is no urgent demand for personal courage, sound nerves or stark beauty, we find ourselves by accident... You can go through contemporary life fudging and evading, indulging and slacking, never really hungry nor frightened nor passionately stirred... your first real contact with primary and elemental necessities, the sweat of your deathbed.

— H.G. WELLS, *Tono-Bungay*

This chapter's practice is inviting difficulty into your life. Let me explain by telling a story from my other "gig," coaching high school soccer.

One windy and cold October afternoon, I was standing next to another soccer coach watching our high school team do sprints. They were already in good physical shape. The goal with these sprints was emotional.

While they were running, the other coach leaned toward me and said, "I think part of our job is to teach kids pain: What is real pain and what is just being uncomfortable. I don't think a lot of them know the difference."

We wanted our young athletes to explore the boundaries of their abilities. To push through discomfort and discover they could keep going. To know what it feels like to reach your maximum heart rate. To realize being sore is different from being injured. Through practice, athletes increase their ability to deal with pain and stress. They know the "can't catch my breath" moment after an anaerobic session will pass, that soreness will fade and injuries will heal.

By inviting difficulty during practice, athletes learn to be tough when it counts. In a game, they are ready to perform at their highest level and meet any challenge.

Being tough is a requirement for any competitive athlete. A sixteen-year-old soccer player reminded me of this a few years ago. Halfway through a game, he came off the field after being kicked in the nose. His nose was split open, lacerated from the bridge to the tip, and his face was covered in blood. I thought, *Well, he's done for a couple weeks.* Our trainer took him aside and used butterfly bandages to close the laceration.

Five minutes later, he was standing by me. Swollen nose, still a little bloody, covered with bandages. "I'm ready to go!"

I said, "No way! You're done!"

He replied, "I'm fine coach, please, let me play!"

So I did. He went back in, played the rest of the game, scored two goals. But the real victory was a young man meeting adversity, pushing through pain, and not falling apart even when he suffered a setback. He continued even when it was hard.

Life isn't so different from soccer.

We need to be tough, and becoming tough takes practice.

It only takes a year or so on the fire department to see this is true. New firefighters on their first calls are still discovering their abilities, their limits and boundaries. How much they can carry, how long they can go, what sort of emotional trauma they can handle. In time, they can carry more, work longer, deal with the most shattering moments.

This requires toughness. To live the lives we want and thrive through the pain that the universe will throw at us, we need to temper our constitutions like athletes.

Do What's Difficult

Is there some activity you've always wanted to do or goal you've wanted to achieve — learn a musical instrument or a new language, run the Boston Marathon, lose thirty pounds — but have put off because it seems too difficult? Do that. Don't worry about whether you will succeed. Focus on an important goal and learn the lessons of how to push through discomfort and pain.

For me, I joined a gym. I had reached my sixties, and my body wasn't as strong or agile anymore. I wanted to make sure I would be physically able to put on my bunker gear at 3 AM, climb into one of our engines, and be useful at a fire. All I wanted was to get in better shape, but the gym taught me a lot about toughness.

First, I noticed that every time I walked into the gym I

was anxious. When I read the "workout of the day" on the board, I'd often think, *I can't do this!* I'd immediately begin planning escape routes. *My knees hurt, I'm tired!* Somehow, I was always cajoled into starting, in part because of a big sign that read, "Stop complaining and start!" Then at the end of some of the most horrible, terrible workouts I'd ever had, my anxiety level was so high I had to stand outside until I could breathe again, until I knew I was going to live and aliens weren't trying to eat their way out of my lungs. This went on for a while.

Yet while I floundered, the maniacs in the gym often had the opposite reaction to strenuous workouts. They would cheer. They got excited. They were obviously brain damaged, twisted. Then I had an insight: The actual point of working out is to overcome that voice that says, *I can't do this!* Every time, the goal is to push yourself out of your comfort zone.

Yes, the hard nature of each workout developed physical fitness, but by doing difficult things, I also developed more emotional toughness. By routinely pushing through discomfort, I learned how to stay stronger and work better in any difficult situation. This was a revelation — our family motto for generations has been, "All things considered, we'd rather nap."

Here are the strategies I learned to help develop toughness.

1. Manage Your Self-Talk: Part One

Listen to what you say to yourself as you confront something difficult. When you hear that voice that says, *I can't do this!*, perhaps the most crucial, critical, and important thing you can do is to stop and question it. Ask: Is that rational? Is that true?

Of course, there are things we cannot do. But we can distinguish doubt and fear from a genuinely impossible task. That voice has little to do with our limits. It arises whenever things become uncomfortable, but discomfort is not a limit. It is not a sign of the apocalypse.

Instead, say to yourself, *This will be hard, maybe extremely difficult, but I'll try*. The difference is more than semantics. If we say, "I can't," everything stops. We turn away. If we say, "I'll try," we allow ourselves to start and see where our limits truly are.

2. Focus on Starting, Not Finishing

Don't think, *Oh my God, I could never run twenty-six miles!* Or, *I could never write a book*. Just begin.

The German novelist Hermann Hesse wrote, "In all beginnings dwells a magic force for guarding us and helping us to live." When we start something, there is the energy of the "new." There is excitement, anxiety, maybe a little fear. Those are the emotions of being outside your comfort zone, of being alive! That is what Hesse meant. Magic forces are there to help. Everyone worries about failing, but who cares if you might fail? Get over it! Anything worth doing is worth failing at a few times. The truth is most people don't even start because they don't want to fail or look stupid. So clear your mind and focus on beginning. Magic will come.

3. Break Hard Stuff Down into Manageable Chunks

Don't allow yourself to be overwhelmed by the entire task. At the gym, while the maniacs are doing fifty burpees, I focus on doing five, or two. If I get through five, then maybe I do five more. Maybe rest in between. Eventually, I've done fifty. One day at a time. One task at a time. Set a pace for yourself, then push it a little bit. In Alcoholics Anonymous, the goal is not to be sober for a lifetime; the goal is to be sober today, or for the next hour. Same with any big task. Break it down into manageable chunks. Five burpees at a time.

4. Manage Your Self-Talk: Part Two

I often tell myself, *Don't go batshit in your brain*. In the middle of hard stuff — I don't know another way to put this — we need to clamp down on our thinking, on what we say to ourselves, and do what needs to be done.

At a bad car crash, with all sorts of people storming around yelling, firefighters learn to shut out all the voices except those of their fellow firefighters. "Focus on the work," one grizzled old captain told me once. It is the same anytime we are attempting something difficult and outside our comfort zone: Mute all the voices in your head that tell you, *It's too hard! I can't, I'll get hurt, I'll look stupid!* Stay focused on the work.

5. Manage Your Self-Talk: Part Three

What if, as we train for our futures, we said to ourselves, *Cool! This is going to be hard!* What if our response to difficulty on the horizon, to all the daily irritants and uncomfortable moments, was to say: *Yes! Something even more difficult! That's just what I need!*

Believe me, nothing was stranger than when the gym maniacs would high-five one another when they saw a challenging workout on the board. Now I get it. They were inviting difficulty into their lives to become physically and emotionally stronger. In fact, there is nothing like accomplishing something difficult to make you feel better about yourself.

The Hard Is What Sculpts Us

Think of your life. The easy stuff isn't what you remember or what shaped you. What sculpted you, what is seared in your memory, is the hard stuff, the battles that you fought, the difficult defeats and arduous victories, the scars of battle. Firefighters don't remember the easy calls. We remember the difficult ones, the ones that tested us, the ones that overwhelmed us or forced us to rise to the occasion and do things we'd never done before.

Embrace difficulty, seek out what is hard; this is how we grow into our true selves.

Because I live in the mountains, I think of embracing difficulty each time Laurie and I hike. In front of us, the peaks are shrouded in mist; we have no idea how high or treacherous the climb will be. But with every step we take, every foot of elevation we gain, even as our legs ache, we get stronger, leaner, and tougher. The rest of the civilized world may linger comfortably in the valley below, but our task is to climb above the mists and see the world. It is worth every step.

Choose the difficult path. Choose the hard way.

Field Notes: On Being Tough

1. Make a list of some of the most difficult things you've endured. They could be physical or emotional challenges.

2. Next to each event, note how the event changed you, in terms of increasing your ability to deal with pain or discomfort, either physical or emotional.

3. For events that are still painful, or that you find difficult to be objective about, imagine you are sitting with a good friend or a therapist. Imagine what they might say. You may feel wounded, or that you "failed," but consider the ways those challenges have made you stronger. That is the goal.

4. This, as hard as it may seem, is the growth path. We go through hard situations. We let some time pass. We analyze how it changed us, and then we move on to something harder, or something more difficult comes our way. But we are tougher.

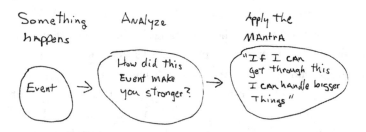

Something happens   Analyze   Apply the Mantra

Event → How did this Event make you stronger? → "If I can get through this I can handle bigger Things"

CHAPTER TWENTY-EIGHT

THE BLUE-HAZED PRAIRIE

I am riding on a limited express, one of the crack
    trains of the nation.
Hurtling across the prairie into blue haze and
    dark air go fifteen all-steel coaches holding a
    thousand people.
(All the coaches shall be scrap and rust and all the
    men and women laughing in the diners and
    sleepers shall pass to ashes.)
I ask a man in the smoker where he is going and
    he answers: "Omaha."

— CARL SANDBURG, "Limited"

This poem by Carl Sandburg sums up a larger firefighter lesson. I read it in high school and later as an adult, and it still keeps banging around in my brain, so that must mean something.

Here is what it means to me: With a sense of self-importance, we each believe that we are headed to Omaha. We believe that we are special and have a unique seat on the train. We sometimes think we are so important in the scheme of things that we are invulnerable, that we are protected from the vicissitudes that drown others.

The truth is that life can be taken from us in a second. The car skids. The woman clutches her chest and goes to her knees. The impulsive child takes the gun to his head. Everything can change in a day. No one is protected. There is no warning, no portents. Crows and ravens do not circle your home on the appointed day. Life is just going on around you, and then, you're dead. Death can devour us just like that.

Second, much of what we have been told is essential about life isn't. We spend our lives struggling, striving, jostling for prizes that in the end turn out to be made of sand. They slip through our fingers. Getting to Omaha is just not what it's cracked up to be.

Third, we are here for such a short time against the backdrop of the infinite, then gone forever: It's a hard truth.

Granted, even after a near-death experience, it takes the reflective power of a Buddhist monk to hold on to these insights. It is hard to hold the truths that we could die tomorrow and turn to rust and ashes, that what we've been led to believe is important is not, and that our life is an astonishingly short blink in time.

Yes, it's been pointed out to me a million times that society would collapse if we solely worried about the universe and our place in it. Laurie once found me moping in the kitchen and asked me what I was doing. I responded with how much I loved her and the kids and how much I would miss them when I died. There was a beat and then she reminded me that it was my turn to take the recycling to the dump.

Ignoring Laurie's practicality for a moment, I cannot help but believe that we would all be happier, more fulfilled, and kinder to one another if we allowed these larger truths to resonate, to become a permanent part of our thinking.

In that spirit, I have an alternative point of view.

It's the other lesson I take from "Limited." Right now, hold the realization that, in this instant, you're alive. It's astonishing really, a revelation: Life is a miraculous confluence of events. Whatever your understanding of the word *miraculous*, to me it means an incredibly low-probability event. We are talking big numbers here; an infinite universe, an endless number of combinations, and yet here we are. Wow. It makes you think.

By any definition, it is a terrible mistake to take this miracle for granted, even for one moment, one instant. Thus, instead of sitting, dreaming of how important we are and how vital it is to get to Omaha, we should press our hands and faces against the window and be astonished by the blue-hazed prairie.

On certain days I understand this. I look at the New Mexico sky and think it's the most beautiful blue I've ever seen, shockingly blue, deliriously blue. Hearing my wife and daughters laugh together is, without doubt, the most lovely music I've ever heard.

I choose to believe that our lives, if we are willing to do the work, have meaning. I choose this because we are sentient human beings; curious, loving, and intelligent. We each are on this planet to create meaning and then live it. Often it takes a couple of false starts and a couple of careers, and what we find meaningful might not fit society's definition of what we should do, be, or have. Often, we mope around for years, pissing off lovers and spouses as we try to figure out why we are here and what the hell we are supposed to do. Spouses want practical answers, and we want existential answers, but you need both. In any regard, the search is imperative. Life without meaning is wandering in the desert. Life with a purpose makes sense. It is that simple.

I've been lucky. I resisted the whole firefighter thing in the beginning. I thought, *Who has the time? I'm goin' to Omaha!* Plus it's a lot of work. There is the blood, suffering, and the claustrophobia of being in a hot, small room with the dragon. Who needs it! Yet ultimately I was pulled in, and it turned out that, other than being a father, being a firefighter has given me more meaning than anything else I've ever done. Being a firefighter gave me a purpose that nothing else had; not work, not play, not money.

It's obvious why this is true, and it's so simple: Nothing is more meaningful than helping others. In the Talmud, it's written that all men are responsible for one another. Albert Schweitzer wrote, "The only ones among you who will be truly happy are those who will have sought and found how to serve." No doubt true. All I know is that it makes me happy. When we've fought a fire, treated a sick patient, or extricated someone from a wrecked car, I feel like I've done something worthwhile. I'll take that any day.

A final metaphor. In the Rocky Mountain forests, like those above my hometown of Santa Fe, there are beautiful stands of aspen. From a distance, they are tall and majestic, iridescently green in the summer rains. But walk through the forests and look more closely. Many of the aspens are bent and crooked. Some have a U shape in the middle of their trunk. This happens because, at some point when the tree was a sapling, its growth was blocked by a boulder. The aspen had to grow around it, and it kept that deformity. But aspens keep growing toward the sun and digging their roots deeper into the soil. It is their daily task.

Evolution's instructions are not "grow straight or die." Nature has programmed aspens to grow, to overcome, and to push skyward. That this is also true for us is self-evident. Our nature is to grow, overcome obstacles, and keep growing. We might look a tangled mess as we get older, we might have great hollows in our trunks caused by sadness and loss, but we have a responsibility to grow and to thrive. It is what we do. This is because we are human; we are the sons and daughters of generations of survivors going back hundreds of thousands of years. Our responsibility — to them, to ourselves, to our children — is to never give in to despair. Keep the spark lit, keep the seedling alive, dig our roots into the ground, and keep growing toward the sun.

THE OLDEST FIRE DEPARTMENT IN THE WEST

It was a big fire in a small neighborhood.

Paul yelled from the cab of the engine, "They've re-paged the county for more help. This fire has got everyone spooked!"

Woody and I were dragging hose and wetting a line parallel with the road on the southern flank of the fire. This would hopefully help stop the spread of the fire. One of our wildfire engines roared past us going up the road, lights flashing off the smoke.

I tied a bandanna over my face to help with the smoke. Paul yelled to us again, "We don't have enough crews to protect houses! We're supposed to let them burn and focus on knocking down the wildfire!"

"Well, I hope everybody got out," Woody grunted, throwing the line over his shoulder.

"Ya," I panted.

We walked up another hundred yards until we came to a driveway. The fire had already blown past this house. The house seemed untouched but was surrounded by blackened, smoking ground. We dragged our line past it.

"Hey," Woody pointed toward the house. "Look."

I looked. Flames were licking up the east side of the garage.

"We can knock that down," he said.

I waved at Paul to get his attention. We both pointed at the garage wall. Paul shrugged. Technically, we were disobeying orders, but spiritually we knew a couple of minutes and some water would save this house.

Grabbing a spare line off the engine, we connected it and dragged it to the garage. It only took a few blasts, but we knocked down the fire. It would later flare up again and a mop-up crew would deal with it, but that house was saved.

Paul yelled at us, "They need us! Just drop the line and let's go!"

We walked back to the engine, uncoupled the line that stretched across the driveway, and climbed back into the cab.

I then noticed we were three of the oldest guys on the department. I was sixty-five, Woody was sixty-eight, and Paul seventy. We had just saved a house!

Woody read my mind. "And they say we're too old! Ha!"

High fives all around. The radio ended our celebration. It was our chief, Tom.

"Engine Two, they need you up higher on the flank. Adam is asking for firefighters."

We flew up the hill, lights and sirens on.

Now, dear reader, if you are thinking the fundamental question why — as in, "Why is a sixty-five-year-old guy out fighting wildfires?"— it's a fair question, and one my wife, friends, and occasionally my therapist ask me.

Let me explain. A friend recently texted me that it takes a lot of courage to get older. I think what she means is that everything is harder. It's hard to wake up from a dream in which you're eighteen and then open your eyes and realize that you're old. It's harder to do simple tasks that you've been doing for a lifetime. Hands stop working. The cold bothers. It's nigh on hysterically funny to watch me try to get into bunker gear at 2 AM. It's not a two-minute drill anymore; it's leaning against a wall, sitting down, and pulling on pants. Of course, looming in the now-more-closer-than-ever future is frailty and the "Big D."

I find being in my midsixties to have a bittersweet quality. I am excruciatingly aware of time passing. My memories illuminate my consciousness more than my dreams of the future.

Yet this is the time, this is the age, that Dylan Thomas wrote about: "Rage, rage against the dying of the light." If it takes courage to grow older, this is the time to summon that courage. This is the time to be fearless, outspoken, to dance unabashedly at college reunions.

This is the time!

Right?

My mother, who is only seventeen years older than I, recently broke her hip, had surgery, and ended up in a rehabilitation center. Everyone there is kind to her; they are compassionate but insistent. There is a schedule, and you have to stick to it. Breakfast at 7:30 AM. Physical therapy at 9 AM, and so on and so on. If not for the Schedule, there would be institutional chaos, my mother has explained to me with more than a touch of sarcasm. Independence is gone. The ability to get up in the middle of the night and have ice cream is gone. She doesn't want to be a burden to the family, but she is terrified of being warehoused someplace where this becomes her life.

That hip fracture, that bout of pneumonia, those first hints of dementia, and the loss of independence are out there in the future. I get it. I don't dwell on it, but it sure makes me appreciate the now, it makes me defiantly want to dance at that college reunion in front of mortified college kids.

And it definitely keeps me on the fire department. In my own way, I want to be useful for as long as I can stretch it out, on as many late-night fires or middle-of-the-day wildfires as I can.

We fought the wildfire I describe above through the evening. We lost two houses but saved six. No one was killed or hurt. A good day, all in all.

As we drove down the flank, looking up the slope, all we could see was blackened ground. A few wildland trucks were patrolling, putting out spot fires. The road was clogged with residents wanting to return home, media trucks, and fire equipment from every district in our region.

"Hey," Paul said as we walked to the command truck, "we're going to be on the news again."

"I just want to go to bed," I said. "Have a drink, have a shower. Sleep and not get up until I feel no pain in my legs."

Adam, our medical captain, met us at the command truck. I sat down next to him, leaned over, and whispered, "If I sit too long, I won't be able to move."

REEEE! "Hondo, Med 80, respond to possible cardiac arrest. Eighteen-year-old male. Unresponsive, not breathing. At 12 Camino Altezita. Time out 19:46."

Adam looked at me. "That's only two miles away, and it sounds more interesting than sitting here."

I replied, "I'm in."

We got up, waved goodbye to the battalion commander.

We jumped — well, Adam jumped and I kinda limped over — to his truck. We took off, lights on and sirens blaring.

Strangely, sitting in the truck, being sixty-five and going sixty-five down the highway, talking about cardiac arrest protocols, I felt great.

I thought to myself, *Just let me be useful one more day.*

ACKNOWLEDGMENTS

The notion that writing a book is a solitary affair is far from the truth. To bring a book from idea to publication is a collaborative effort, and I had great collaborators.

Laurie Wilson, my wife and fellow firefighter (retired), gave me the idea for the book. Laurie Harper of Author Biz Consulting put me on the right track. Jody Rein, my agent, coach, and thinking partner (jodyreinbooks.com), guided me through the arduous process of outlining, writing proposals, being rejected, and finally finding a publisher who was enthusiastic about the book. That person is Jason Gardner, my editor at New World Library. Jason, Jeff Campbell, and the team at New World have been supportive and creative. The highest praise I can give is that I have learned a lot, and I am in their debt.

Next, I had great early readers of the book. Tracy Burke, Terri Pitts, Linda Pedalty, and Terry Protheroe all helped shape my thinking.

My daughter Sullivan Wilson helped with designing the Field Notes in the book.

Finally, I had the great fortune of having the artwork of Dan Bodelson illuminate the book. Dan (danbodelson.com), besides having been a great firefighter, is an iconic Santa Fe artist. His paintings are luminous and capture the beauty of our home, Santa Fe.

ABOUT THE AUTHOR

For over thirty years, Hersch Wilson has been a volunteer firefighter-EMT with the Hondo Fire Department in Santa Fe County, New Mexico. He is also a storyteller, committed to explaining how first responding can change how we see and experience our own lives. He is also a writer, speaker, and consultant. In the past twenty-five years, Hersch has worked extensively with leadership teams from a variety of organizations, including Kodak, IBM Japan, Altria, the US Postal Service, the CIA, Kraft Foods, and Baxter, to name a few. He has cowritten three national business bestsellers with Larry Wilson, including the award-winning *Play to Win!: Choosing Growth Over Fear in Work and Life.*

Hersch attended Colorado College, and he graduated with a BA in English from the University of Minnesota. Prior to becoming a writer and consultant, Hersch was a dancer. He performed in Canada, Switzerland, and the United States. He has also worked as a commercial pilot and a soccer coach.

Hersch and his ex-firefighter wife, Laurie, have two daughters, Brynne and Sully, and one granddaughter, Fiona Scout. They have a house full of dogs, with two Bernese mountain dogs, Nellie and Tank, and one rescue terrier-Chihuahua named Maisie. Hersch writes a monthly column on dogs for the *Santa Fe New Mexican.*

www.herschwilson.com